BRIGHT NOTES

THE TRIAL AND OTHER WORKS BY FRANZ KAFKA

Intelligent Education

Nashville, Tennessee

BRIGHT NOTES: The Trial and Other Works
www.BrightNotes.com

No part of this publication may be used or reproduced in any manner whatsoever without written permission, except in the case of brief quotations in critical articles and reviews. For permissions, contact Influence Publishers http://www.influencepublishers.com.

ISBN: 978-1-645421-32-0 (Paperback)
ISBN: 978-1-645421-33-7 (eBook)

Published in accordance with the U.S. Copyright Office Orphan Works and Mass Digitization report of the register of copyrights, June 2015.

Originally published by Monarch Press.
Gregor Roy, 1966
2020 Edition published by Influence Publishers.

Interior design by Lapiz Digital Services. Cover Design by Thinkpen Designs.

Printed in the United States of America.

Library of Congress Cataloging-in-Publication Data forthcoming.
Names: Intelligent Education
Title: BRIGHT NOTES: The Trial and Other Works
Subject: STU004000 STUDY AIDS / Book Notes

CONTENTS

1) Introduction to Franz Kafka — 1

2) Short Works of Kafka — 37

3) The Metamorphosis — 46

4) A Country Doctor — 57

5) In The Penal Colony — 65

6) The Trial — 72

7) The Castle — 82

8) Amerika — 98

9) Commentary — 105

10) Essay Questions and Answers — 113

11) Bibliography — 118

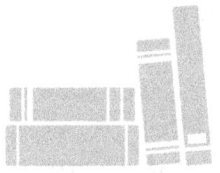

FRANZ KAFKA

INTRODUCTION

BIOGRAPHY: GENERAL OUTLINE

Franz Kafka was born in Prague on July 3, 1883, into a middle-class Jewish family. After receiving his doctorate in law in 1906 at the German University, he worked for the Austrian government in a job dealing with workmen's compensation. He grew up with an increasing sense of inadequacy, mainly due to his father's dominant personality, and this factor contributed greatly to his failure to get married. Falling into ill health, he spent a considerable time in various sanatoriums. His official position with the government prevented his participation in the First World War, but he nevertheless suffered a great deal of privation due to the conflict. A brief romance in 1923 with a young Jewish girl named Dora Dymant gave him a touch of short-lived happiness. On June 3, 1924, he died of tuberculosis at Klosterneuburg.

HIS WORKS

Kafka worked slowly and painstakingly at his writing, and as a result it was almost impossible for him to make a living solely from his works. Many of his works were, in fact, published after his death. These include *Der Prozess* (1925: Eng. translation, *The Trial*, 1937), *Das Schloss* (1926; Eng. translation, *The Castle*, 1930), and *Amerika* (1927; Eng. translation, *Amerika*, 1938). He also wrote many stories, the most important of which are "A Hunger-Artist", "In the Penal Colony", "A Country Doctor", "The Judgement", and "The Metamorphosis". Although Kafka's works are generally recognized as being difficult and sometimes even impossible to understand completely, they are written in a prose style often marked by precision and lucidity. There is a dreamlike quality about the world created by Kafka's imaginative genius, but it is nevertheless a world which is also frighteningly real. In this world, modern man is depicted as a creature beleaguered by fear, haunted by guilt, and burdened by anxiety; an alienated and isolated figure who is engaged in a perpetual but futile quest for salvation. The clarity of his style belies the complex and obscure allegorical elements which enmesh his plots. Kafka places his lonely figures against a background of surrealist dreams, yet one shrouded in an atmosphere of chilling reality.

The Scottish poet and scholar Edwin Muir, who first translated many of Kafka's works, made an interesting comparison, for example, between *The Castle* and *Pilgrim's Progress*. He pointed out, however, the major difference between the two works: namely, that the hero of Bunyan's allegory knew where he was going, and the hero of Kafka's work didn't. The hardships which beset the seventeenth-century Christian could be met with a fortitude born of a deep faith in man's spiritual destiny; the obstacles which prevent Kafka's from reaching his destination, however, take the form of forces incomprehensible to modern man. Moreover, Kafka's hero does not understand the nature of his destination, nor can he come to terms with the reasons for his failure.

Kafka has been described as an extremely moral writer, one who sees the human dilemma in terms of man as the victim of a skeptical age, bewildered and alone, yet struggling with a noble futility to fulfill some divine injunction he cannot understand. Before embarking on a detailed analysis of his works, we shall examine some aspects of Kafka's biography which necessarily throw some measure of light on his personality and art.

EARLY LIFE AND FAMILY BACKGROUND

As we have seen, Franz Kafka was born on July 3, 1883, and was the son of a well-to-do Czech Jewish merchant, Hermann Kafka, a successful and imposing man who exercised a strong influence on the writer throughout his life. The father's indomitable spirit, patriarchal philosophy, and sense of sacrifice formed a continual source of inspiration for Franz in his creative career. The adulation with which he regarded his father was all-important in his early emotional development, but contained exaggerated elements suggesting a certain imbalance which was possibly as detrimental as it was salubrious. From his father's side, Franz received a sense of vitality and capacity for living which seemed to be a hereditary characteristic.

Franz's mother, on the other hand, was a sensitive, quiet, and extremely intelligent woman whose family background was marked by more scholarly, romantic and even reclusive elements. Franz was the eldest of six children, two of whom died in childhood. There was a considerable gap in years between Franz and his three sisters, and his early years were marked by extremely painful loneliness. He received his primary education from governesses and in schools which were both uninspiring and unimaginative. Kafka later called the resultant unhappiness and gawkiness "earthweight". His education was German, on both the elementary and grammar school levels, and was of a particularly severe and authoritarian nature. He was a serious student who read a great deal and took little interest in physical activities. Although he made a few friends among his schoolmates-including the philosopher Hugo Bergmann - the strongest impact on Kafka during this period was that made by the image of his father. This paternal influence is worth examining in some detail, not only for its intrinsic biographical interest, but also for the effect it had on Kafka's later writings.

FATHER'S INFLUENCE

In 1919 Kafka wrote a long, complicated document called "Letter to My Father", which throws some light on the complexities of this relationship. Although he intended this work to be given to his father as a means of alleviating what had developed into a distressing state of affairs, this in fact never happened. It is a highly personal and subjective work, and its subject matter was of such immediate importance to Kafka that its contents are for the most part ambiguous and obscure in meaning. Nevertheless, despite the difficult and self-contradictory aspects of this letter, there is a unifying thematic thread running throughout which explains much of Kafka's attitude toward his father and the influence which this attitude had on his writings. Couched in its simplest terms, it is the story of a son's weakness pitted against a father's strength. His father was a man who achieved everything through conscious strength of will, and who set up his own self, with its inviolable fortitude, as the criterion against which all values were to be measured.

There is nevertheless a permeating awareness that the dichotomy of such a relationship is much more complicated than at first appears. For one thing, Kafka inherited conflicting traits from both sides of his family: shyness, sensitivity, and a tendency toward eccentricity on his mother's side: and strength, eloquence, and a feeling of superiority on his father's. These contrasting traits affected Kafka's personality so deeply that he considered them the contributing factor in his inability to get married. He even went as far as to substantiate Dean Swift's dictum that "children should be brought up only away from their families, not by their parents". The irregularities in his father's authoritarian attitude not only had a detrimental effect on Kafka's personality, but also influenced much of his later work. We will note, for example, the value he placed on authority in such works as *The Trial* and *The Castle*.

The boundless esteem with which Kafka regarded his father was met with an almost total inability on the part of the parent-doubtless due to a certain intractable quality of temperament-to understand the unique characteristics of his own son. As a result of Kafka's early inability to match the qualities he so esteemed in his father, the writer harbored feelings of inadequacy and guilt which never left him.

JUDAISM AND KAFKA'S CHILDHOOD

At an early age, Kafka turned to Judaism as an attempted means of eluding the destructive domination of his father's influence. This excursion into the spiritual realm of his heritage had a profound effect on his attitude to his father, and on his later religious life. There were three stages in this development, which can be outlined briefly as follows:

1. An intense feeling of obligation toward the regulations of the Jewish faith, such as regular attendance at the synagogue, obeying the fasting laws, and so on. The guilt

Kafka felt on transgressing the rules of Judaism was based, however, on the deep-rooted feeling of having offended his own father.

2. A growing awareness of the shallow, fragmentary nature of his father's religious beliefs, and a concomitant bewilderment, mingled with hostility, at the paternal reproaches Kafka received whenever he himself showed dissatisfaction with Judaism. Kafka observed more and more that there was a great deal of hypocrisy in his father's attitude to religion. The fact that this hypocrisy was being imposed on him added to his confused and unhappy feelings.

3. An increasingly sympathetic understanding of his father's authoritative attitude toward Kafka's religious obligations, based on a gradual awareness that his father had indeed absorbed many of the deeper aspects of Judaism. He saw that his father believed in the absolute rectitude of a certain business class of the Jewish community, and that a certain historical innocence on his father's part helped to create the reproachful demeanor under which the young Kafka smarted. Kafka was also interested to note that with his own increasing interest in Jewish affairs, philosophy, and literature, there was a corresponding disgust on his father's part with these forms of Judaism. Kafka also became more and more aware of the fact that the father's disgust was actually directed at his own son.

FAMILY LIFE AND INFLUENCE

One main factor which affected Kafka's life and works was the way in which his mother failed to assert herself firmly with his father. This gave Kafka the impression that the family formed a common enemy against him, and the effects of this are found throughout his works. If we remember this fact, a short story such as "The Married Couple" becomes intensely biographical. Yet despite the fact that Kafka was acutely aware of his father's attitude, he continually sought his approval. He even dedicated one of his books, "A Country Doctor", to his father, but even this was not accepted graciously. So Kafka's lifelong sense of alienation found its roots deep in his family life, and this attitude was of course translated into his unsuccessful relationships with schoolmates, teachers, and, later, women.

There has been some controversy as to the reasons for Kafka's ultimate feelings of loss and alienation. Some critics claim that Kafka unwittingly modeled his image of God after his own father, while others hold the opposite to be true: namely, that the image Kafka had of his father became inflated out of all rational proportion as his experience of God and a hostile universe became more deeply entrenched. In any case, what cannot be disputed is that one of the ideas central to Kafka's works is the motif of family responsibility, and all that this concept implies. In "The Metamorphosis", for example, the son's transformation into a loathsome species of vermin is indicative of the effect which Kafka's family background had on his thinking.

UNIVERSITY AND ITS EFFECTS

At university, Kafka decided to study law, since, as he himself stated, the study of law provided him with the widest scope for the indifference he had toward academic subjects. His natural bent was toward creative art, and during this period he developed the idea of leaving Prague and embarking on something entirely different from the academic life. Surprisingly enough, although elements in his works have been compared to the darker side of such writers as Baudelaire and Poe, Kafka leaned more to literature of simplicity and natural emotions during his university days. He was an outstandingly honest and conscientious student, and displayed a deep interest in questions of a moral nature, particularly when any hint of injustice arose. This scrupulous honesty in debating ethics is important to remember when reading *The Trial*, for example. This developing conscientiousness revealed itself later artistically in the attention Kafka paid in his works to precise detail. This fascination for detail is closely linked with his ruthless quest for truth behind the facade commonly called "reality". An inevitable whisper of **irony** is heard in some of his exploratory passages, even in a work such as "In the Penal Colony".

In his student days, he displayed an ingenuous simplicity which belied his profound concern for the paradoxes of human existence. He developed a love for the works of Flaubert and Goethe, and read Plato's *Protagoras*, which he enjoyed for the Socratic **irony** it contains. According to the obituary by the philosopher Bergmann, Kafka in his student days also made a close study of St. Francis of Assisi, the Bible, Luther, the Upanishads, and the *Decameron*. It was during this period that he developed his unique power not only of observing details, but of connecting them to an uncommon degree. This factor is important to remember if we wish to appreciate the symbolism of his works, which he employed to highlight philosophical abstractions.

He received his doctorate in jurisprudence at the Imperial and Royal Karl-Ferdinand German University of Prague on July 18, 1906.

CHOICE OF CAREER: A DILEMMA

Although Kafka had no intention of pursuing a legal career, he spent the mandatory probationary year in the courts to give himself a breathing space in which to decide on his future. Since he himself described writing as "a form of prayer", he rejected the idea of taking any job connected with literature. He obtained a position in an insurance institute, and tried writing in the evening, but with little success. Yet Kafka did learn much about existing social injustices through his contact with workmen, and many of the realistic descriptions contained in *The Trial* and *The Castle* are derived from his experiences at this time. On the whole, however, the daily drudgery of his work grew more and more unbearable until he actually contemplated suicide.

At this time two diametrically opposed tendencies fought for ascendancy in Kafka - the desire for solitude and the need for society. Notice that K., the hero of *The Castle*, strives with desperate futility to achieve the highest goal of life in a social community. While Kafka disapproved of his tendency toward solitude, he realized that it was necessary for the self-absorption needed for writing. During this period he also indulged in much detailed self-examination, and in 1911 made the somewhat startling declaration that he seemed to be totally without feeling. It was as if he were separated from everything around him by what he called "a space to whose limits I can't even force my way out". Again, in 1912, he described himself as being "heartless" because of his literary talents. Yet art for Kafka was a truly religious experience, inasmuch as it is, in his words, "dazzled by the Truth", a function whereby life's meaning can somehow be illuminated, helping man to fulfill his natural abilities.

LITERARY DEVELOPMENT

There followed a period of creative barrenness and lethargy which left Kafka in a mood of near despair. In September 1912, however, he completed his first long story, called "The Verdict", which represented a kind of stylistic "breakthrough" after a spell of doubt and aridity. By this time Kafka had collected a wealth of literary material in the form of diaries, and several publishers expressed interest, if the writer would submit a manuscript. The selections chosen by Kafka were collected and published under the title *Contemplation*. Shortly after this, he started writing his novel *Amerika* and completed his short story "The Metamorphosis".

There are painfully autobiographical elements in his story "The Verdict", which concerns the fate of a loyal and dutiful son who throws himself in a river with a protesting cry of love as a result of being spurned by his own father. In 1913, *Contemplation* appeared; a work remarkable for its prose style alone, containing a simplicity within the complexities of the sentences, and written in evocative and stimulating language. "The Metamorphosis" is a remarkable work inasmuch as Kafka succeeds in revealing the free world which surrounds the horror of its contents. It is also essential to note the legal aspects of a work such as "The Metamorphosis", in which a dreadful sentence is executed upon a man who is imperfect. Kafka's works abound in judgments and punishments. Yet Kafka is not negating life in such works, but is rather highlighting-often in frightening terms - the depths to which man can sink in his inability to elevate himself to God's level. In this period, Kafka completed only the first two chapters of his novel *Amerika*, which is the only one of his works which ends on an optimistic note.

ROMANTIC EPISODE AND FURTHER WRITING

Kafka held the institution of marriage and the patriarchal way of life in the highest esteem, and often expressed a strong personal desire to be a husband and father. Between 1912 and 1914 he engaged in a tortured and hopeless love affair with a girl who awakened in him the realization of the deep-rooted sexual fears he harbored; fears so crippling that he himself said: "The very idea of a honeymoon fills me with horror". Despite the unhappiness of this affair, he continued to labor on at least two of his major works, *The Trial* and "In the Penal Colony", and made a close study of the works of Dostoevsky, Strindberg, and Pascal. During this period, he also made genuine and strenuous efforts to make a clean break from his family, and in 1915 even took a room by himself, where he continued to work intensively on *The Trial*. The causes of his personal misery, ending in his total inability to face marriage, were understandably complex.

Financially, he faced abject poverty if he relied on his pen for a living. On the other hand, he felt artistically ruined by spending his life poring over legal documents. Yet to rely on the financial support of his parents was an equally soul-destroying prospect. But above and beyond these social and financial reasons for his unhappiness, Kafka suffered from a profound psychological and **metaphysical** malaise which found expression in his writings. In 1917 he began to show signs of deteriorating physical health which indicated that he was suffering from tuberculosis. He refused to enter a sanatorium, however, but went instead to live on a small estate at Zurow taken over by his youngest sister. It was here that he began work on one of his greatest books, *The Castle*.

KAFKA AND RELIGION

Kafka stayed at Zurow until 1918, when he returned to Prague and his Civil Service job. He collected the stories which were to become "A Country Doctor" and even insisted on their being published. His religious position at this time is worth examining, since it reflects in many ways a positive love of life rather than a posture of despair and self-abnegation. He was fond of quoting passages from Kierkegaard stressing the moral strength of mankind, and it is important to note that Kafka did recognize that man is not merely the hapless pawn of some super-being upon whose mercy he has been cast. Let us stress, however, that this optimistic attitude hardly ever shows itself in his works, which abound with a sense of man's bewildered and futile struggle against **metaphysical** odds totally incomprehensible to him. It is nonetheless important to recognize that Kafka did have this positive quality in his attitude to religion. His quarrel with God has even been equated with that of Job. Kafka indulged in a perpetual, tortured quest for an answer and a faith which he never found.

Despite the futility of finding a definitive, totally satisfying solution, however, there was in Kafka the belief that man at least does struggle, question, and strive, and that man's active task should be directed toward that which is good, and which concerns life. Kafka believed that for all the imperfections and uncertainties of human activities, there is an Absolute. The tragedy of man's position lies in his inability to perceive and relate to this Absolute for reasons too complex and mysterious for his comprehension. The resultant desperation, misery, despair, and **irony** form part of the thematic structure of such works as *The Castle*, *The Trial*, and "In the Penal Colony". If God is cruel, unjust, and absurd, this is so because God is being judged from man's inhuman position and according to man's inadequate criteria.

FINAL YEARS

In 1923, he met a young Jewish girl, Dora Dymant, with whom he formed a close attachment which lasted and which deepened during the final year of his life. The last winter of his life was nevertheless plagued with unhappiness, much of it due to the postwar inflation and resultant economic distress. His health deteriorated, and he was forced to enter a sanatorium, where it was discovered that he was suffering from tuberculosis of the larynx. In his last days he showed a passionate desire for health and life, prompted to a great extent by the devotion he felt for and received from Dora. At the end of his life he also displayed a genuine and moving feeling of affection for his parents, a feeling he expressed in self-controlled terms untainted with any trace of false sentimentality. On his death bed, he worked on the proofs of his final book, "A Hunger-Artist", and even expressed reproach toward his publisher for some mistakes that had been made.

POSTHUMOUS FAME

Kafka died on June 3, and was buried in the Jewish cemetery in Prague. At this point it should be remembered that he died almost totally unknown as a writer, and that recognition of his works and genius came only after his death. Unlike the case of other writers, however, this was due not so much to the callous indifference of the public as to Kafka's own indifference to achieving fame and fortune during his lifetime. His ambitions were directed more to an inner spiritual perfection, for which he strove with a driving intensity expressed brilliantly in his writings. Much of his personal pain and wretchedness was caused by a growing realization on his part of the weaknesses in his nature which formed constant stumbling blocks between himself and fusion with the divine being he referred to as the "Indestructible".

As for public reaction to the writer's death and works, it is more than interesting to note that when Kafka's friend and biographer, Max Brod, approached Gerhart Hauptmann concerning the posthumous publication of his writings, the eminent literary figure replied that he had never even heard of Kafka. We have learned a great deal about Kafka's personality, views, and works from close acquaintances of his: from Max Brod himself, for example, from Dora Dymant, who was closest to him at the end of his life, and from a book by Gustav Janouch, who had painstakingly recorded many of Kafka's conversations during his lifetime. There have been many distortions of his image, of course, but it goes without saying that we must turn to his works, rather than to his biographies, to obtain the inner image which is to us, as it was to him, of paramount importance.

Before we proceed to examine his works, however, we shall look briefly at the literary trends and **genres** of German literature in Kafka's period. This will give the student a clearer idea of how his works fit into the general literary patterns of his age and bring him to a better understanding of Kafka's stature as a writer.

Literary Trends

It can safely be said that the intellectual trends of the Wilhelmian period of German literature were on the whole political in nature. Great changes were taking place geographically, psychologically, and politically in Central Europe, and the resultant spiritual and historical upheavals of the age had a marked impact on the cultural climate into which Kafka was born. It was an age of crisis in German history, and the drama of 1870 was proving but a prelude to the tragedy of 1914. In South Germany, there was a marked trend toward sharp **satire** directed against the hypocrisy which had crept into the cultural life of the country. Such writers as Karl Kraus and Ludwig Thoma contributed biting comments on the sham of so much that they saw in contemporary society.

In North Germany, the effect of Nietzsche was felt, particularly in the writings of Paul Ernst (1866-1933) who made a brilliant analysis of the nature and downfall of German idealism. In severe but energetic tragedies such as Canossa and Ariadne auf Naxos, he severely criticized the deterministic cult to which German intellectualism had fallen heir. The contrast between Kafka and Ernst is particularly worthy of note when we remember that Ernst, with his classicist approach, saw literature in the widest political terms. To Ernst, aesthetic-and particularly poetic- values had importance relative to their social effectiveness. This attitude was in some ways unique at that time, but it gradually permeated European thought, eventually finding champions in such voices as Nietzsche and Stefan George.

Fiction at the Turn of the Century

Perhaps the greatest change in the literary tone of the period is found in fiction, where the analytic, self-conscious perceptiveness of poetry found deft and far-reaching expression. It was almost as if novelists were determined to analyze and criticize the chaos and anarchy of the values around them in highly individualistic and skeptical terms. Yet this individualism was but a reflection of the broader aspects of the current cultural vista. In the hypersensitive perceptions of the best novelists of the period, there was a clear-cut recognition of the stagnation which paralyzed much of European intellectual life. This factor is worth remembering when we come to examine in detail the works of Kafka, who translated this mood in terms of man's spiritual dilemma.

One of the most influential literary spokesmen of this period was Ricarada Huch, whose novels and historical studies displayed a neoromantic tendency tempered by scholarly precision and narrative lucidity. Her critical appraisals of the German romantics (Die Romantik) is interesting inasmuch as it was symptomatic of a current tendency among certain of the impressionist novelists: namely, the turning back to past modes and convictions in order to achieve a sense of permanence in their own works. Yet as in all literary movements, there are outstanding exceptions, and in this period the Nobel Prize winner Carl Spitteler stood almost alone in creating a rich atmosphere of myth, verbal rhythm, and poetic power which succeeded in stressing the necessity of individual moral responsibility toward creating a strong social order.

It must be born in mind that Kafka's literary position and cultural development was not divorced from all this; but by understanding the cultural tone of his literary education we can better evaluate his uniqueness and appreciate his genius.

Thomas Mann and the Narrative Tradition

The novels of Thomas Mann reflect not only a tradition of German romanticism, but also a growing concern with the political and social problems of the day. He approached these from the moral and **metaphysical** stance which formed part of his personal cultural creed. It could even be said that there is a Kafka-esque quality about a novel such as *Der Zauberberg*, for example, inasmuch as it concerns the spiritual crisis of a human being-in a sanatorium-trapped by the temptation of irrational reasoning in the face of death. In this novel, Mann captures the essence of the puzzling spiritual patterns of postwar European civilization, and is worth studying in juxtaposition to Kafka's major works. Mann's writings reveal an acuity of perception concerning the moral and cultural problems of European civilization. He owes a great deal in his intellectual position to the thinking of Nietzsche and to traditional German conservatism, yet was very conscious of historical progress and the unique spiritual challenge made by this process. While he felt himself most akin to the tradition of such writers as Heine, Ibsen, Tolstoy and Gide, he also admitted a great debt to Goethe.

Spiritual Concerns of Literature

To appreciate fully the major **metaphysical** aspects of Kafka's works, it cannot be stressed too much that the turn of the century in European literature saw a major concern on the part of writers for a reappraisal of spiritual values. Throughout the intellectual world of Europe there was a sense of the impending collapse of the existing moral order, and this mood was felt most sharply in Germany. In Nietzchean terms, the prevailing mood was one of nihilism, inasmuch as an element of the bourgeois world was speaking in terms of revolt against its own moral order. We must bear in mind at this point that Kafka was the product of the bourgeoisie and therefore belonged in a very real sense to this middle-class awareness of spiritual stagnation and moral disintegration.

This was not a "revolutionary" movement, however, inasmuch as its aim was the amelioration of the existing social order. It was rather an attack on the standards of banality and crassness which formed the basis of middle-class morality, and Nietzsche's diatribes against these standards were part of a general plea for a renaissance of noble values. As the German state intensified its efforts toward a virile and successful self-realization, there grew a concomitant criticism of the resultant grossness of taste. Kafka's literary, intellectual, and spiritual growth took place therefore in an atmosphere of cultural crisis, and we must remember this in our evaluation of his contribution to European intellectual life.

Kafka and the Cultural Crisis

Kafka's position in the cultural upheaval of the age can be appreciated fully only if we are aware of the patterns which affected what has been called the "spiritual coherence" of the times. The First World War came as the explosive **climax** of smoldering nineteenth-century historical complexities, and consequently plunged Germany into a period of political, economic, and social turmoil. The culmination of all this, of course, was the Nazi era and its barbarism, so it is not surprising to find post-Second World War German writers facing problems of spiritual self-analysis remarkably similar to their earlier counterparts. In this sense, therefore, one cannot safely talk of a clear-cut development along neatly defined lines.

What one can see, however, is the dual aspects of a spiritual crisis on the one hand, and a desperate search for an ordered pattern of faith on the other. The plight of Kafka's heroes becomes more understandably desperate when we realize that Kafka himself spent his creative years in a similar historical situation. Philosophically, the mood of the whole era was analyzed, synthesized, and challenged by the radicalism of Nietzsche, whose works and thought were unfortunately made the victim of vicious and pernicious misinterpretation. Generally speaking, Nietzsche's work invokes a demanding examination of the reasons for the spiritual torpor which blighted the times.

From a different perspective, Oswald Spengler attempted something similar by interpreting history in terms of complex spiritual upheavals. The fact of Spengler's world vision being negative and pessimistic is in itself testimony to the intellectual malaise of the age. In art, painters like Franz Marc displayed an inner intensity, almost approaching ecstasy, which was an expressionistic manifestation of the soul-searching which marked the temper of the age. In poetry, there was an upsurge of lyrical energy often directed against the dehumanizing effects of the age of machines. The works of Ernst Barlach, for example, contain powerful lyrical expressions of a deep religious mysticism which was also part of the same involuted spiritual quest. The prose of the period was deeply affected by all these trends, but particularly by Nietzsche's penetrating questionings and by Freud's revelations concerning the symbolism of man's explicit activities. And no writer of the period embraced and epitomized these elements more brilliantly or stirringly than Franz Kafka.

Themes

In Kafka's work there is a blending of the neoromantic and the surrealistic, the spiritual and the realistic, the allegorical and the symbolical, all fused in a stylistic lucidity most remarkable when we consider the underlying complexities. The dominant **theme** of his major works is the almost unbearable sense of human isolation and the tragedy of man's exclusion from a spiritual home whose nature he cannot comprehend. Man is depicted as a creature riddled with guilt whose life is a kind of legal trial dominated by a universe he cannot fathom. God to Kafka is a patriarchal, Jehovah-like presence, at once terrifying and awe-inspiring. There is a lack of consolation for his characters, who are like puppets trapped and frustrated by a sense of cosmic incoherence. The law is of paramount importance in Kafka's works. Symbolized by the police, government officials, the castle, and so on, the law is forever present to remind man of his crime-although he does not know the reality of the crime. What he does know, however, is the reality of his guilt, which paralyzes his every move.

Influences

Apart from the historical influences we have discussed, Kafka was deeply affected by the Talmud and by his background in Jewish literature. His thinking has also been strongly linked to that of Pascal, and his philosophy to the existentialism of Kierkegaard. There are obvious parallels, in his religious attitudes, to the plays of Strindberg and the novels of Dostoevsky. The influence of surrealism is seen in his continual use of landscapes set in a dream world of fantastic phenomena, the details of which Kafka describes with a remarkable degree of precision.

Kafka was very representative of his age also in his social awareness. His characters are social animals too, locked in the deluding **realism** of their bourgeois existence. And even in the deceptive security of the world they inhabit, they are forever aware of the fact that they are out of touch with this social milieu. Their dilemma is therefore not only spiritual and **metaphysical**, but also social, compounded by the fact that they are purblind to the possibility of survival or even of annihilation.

Let us make clear at this point, however, something we touched on earlier, namely, that there is ever-present an element of hope. It is only faintly discernible, but it is nevertheless there, inasmuch as there is an indefinable faith in Kafka's "Indestructible". Even in the most absurd and grotesque spiritual plights in which his characters find themselves, the fact of their "hanging on" is in itself testimony to the mysterious quality of defiance which exists in them despite their sense of moral and social enslavement. If we consider in itself the fact that Kafka depicted man's plight, perplexities and doubts so realistically and in **metaphysical** terms so uncannily realistic, and that he posed questions immediate in their dramatic intensity and ultimate in their moral importance, he must be considered one of the most profoundly religious writers of the century.

Kafka and Realism

One perfectly valid criterion for judging any novel is the extent to which the author has succeeded in giving us a plausible and effective depiction of society. The novels of Jane Austen, for example, present a realistic portrait of a highly stylized segment of her environment. Dickens and Thackeray on the whole did much the same thing, though on a more sweeping scale. Much of the activity and behavior is externalized and depicted as events happening outside, and reported by the story-teller. In the history of the French novel, for example, the names Flaubert and Balzac are almost automatically associated with what we would normally call "realism".

German fiction, however, does not have the same "realistic" roots as does that of France, despite the works of such mid-nineteenth-century German writers as Gotthelf and Keller. Even in Goethe's *Wilhelm Meister* - often cited as a realistic novel - there are strong elements of the demonic. The traditional cult of non-realism in German fiction may be attributed in part to the nature of German Romanticism, with its failure to embrace all the forms, aspects, and activities of the world its writers belonged to. When a writer deliberately loses complete grip of the social experiences around him, and plunges entirely into the world of introspective fantasy for his **themes** - as many of the German Romantics did - he falls into grave danger of artistic mediocrity and even dishonesty.

The trend in German fiction after the turn of the century- to which Kafka fell heir-was a neoromantic one in which novelists used symbols, myths, and leitmotifs to heighten their depiction of man and his dilemma. In the nineteen-twenties, for example, novelists attempted to move into dimensions of activity less objective and clearly defined than their nineteenth-century counterparts. Two of the best examples of this trend are James Joyce's *Ulysses* and Franz Kafka's *The Castle*, which, although obviously more vocatively brilliant than the novels of the German Romantics, were nevertheless part of the same tradition. By going beyond the frontiers of **realism**, they move into a world of vague, ill-defined shadows which are nevertheless vividly portrayed for us. It is as if writers like Joyce and Kafka were really giving us a bold vision of the "real" unreality which lies behind, beneath, and beyond what was the real world to a Dickens or a Thackeray. The earlier, or more traditional type of novel has been described as giving a realistic, photographic depiction of life, while the novels of Joyce or Kafka X-ray the real world in surrealistic terms.

Kafka and Expressionism

Expressionism may be defined briefly as an art form in which the artist deliberately and skillfully distorts the outer manifestations of nature in order to highlight the vision he has of the inner world. It is actually a process of aesthetic transformation, by which externals are interpreted in terms of internal realities beyond man's total comprehension. In art, such painters as Ensor, Van Gogh, and Gauguin were precursors of the movement, while in the novel, Kafka and Joyce are the principal pioneers. In fiction such as *The Castle* and *Ulysses*, there is an implicit revolt against naturalism and **realism**, a revolt expressed by a sense of exploration into psychological, spiritual, and **metaphysical** areas untouched by the earlier type of novel. In the years before and after the First World War, literary expressionism took a radical form expressed in a kind of ecstasy aimed at exposing the artist's vision of the inner world together with an acute social awareness. In this respect, Franz Kafka stands head and shoulders above his contemporaries. His novels and stories revealed to contemporary writers the great possibilities inherent in the use of symbolism alone. He also achieved the fantastically difficult task of fusing the real world with the world of dreams, while simultaneously depicting man's spiritual and **metaphysical** loneliness in terms of fear and guilt.

There have of course been many conflicting interpretations of Kafka's meaning and method. Some critics have seen his works in an almost demonic light, depicting man as perpetually damned in a hell designed by some malignant deity. Others take a purely religious view of his writings, claiming that his central figures depict man's indomitable quest for God. On the other hand, some commentators read his works in Freudian terms alone, interpreting every character and incident as artistic expressions of the writer's own abnormal psychological structure. It has even been suggested that Kafka actually had no clear-cut purpose in mind apart from being deliberately obscure, leaving open the possibility of many valid solutions to the puzzles presented by his works. Yet despite what we have said about Kafka's expressionistic explorations into dimensions beyond reality, the reader must ask himself what the realities contained in his novels are in fact. And the answer is that his works have the realities of burning sincerity, intense anguish, and tortured seeking. They are the precise and detailed accounts of a vision of mankind viewed from an introspective world fraught with the pain of isolation and the eternal plea for a solace which Kafka himself never found.

Kafka and Society

Kafka's works have also been interpreted as being an artistic expression of his acute social-political awareness. While this is by no means the whole picture of his intention, it nevertheless opens up the question of Kafka's views of and relationship to society. He was himself extremely pessimistic about the possibility of the artist's ever being accorded the full status in society which he deserves. We have already seen how his own personal position, in financial terms alone, was made even more anguished by his sense of dependency on the support of his family. He expresses the dilemma of the artist's role in society very poignantly in a short story called "Josephine the Singer". Josephine, whose function in the mousestate is to express the sentiments of the mouse people in song, is rejected when she suggests that she be made exempt from the normal chores expected of her. At this point we should point out the tremendous sense of rapport Kafka had personally with lonely and sensitive people, irrespective of their artistic temperaments. Kafka saw it as humanity's duty to comfort and help the lonely and the suffering, and was, of course, acutely aware of the artist's plight in this respect. And in the society he saw around him, he found little if any public sympathy or aid for the artist. This doubtless led to a strong tendency toward pessimism in his works regarding the norms and taste set by the materialistic society he saw around him. This pessimism was justified, however, particularly when we realize that Kafka was motivated in his thinking by standards of justice, truth and human decency. It is important to remember that the hero of *The Castle* is a social being alienated from the community around him as well as a symbol of man isolated from a religious experience he craves but cannot comprehend.

Now it is true, as has often been pointed out, that in his novels Kafka carefully avoids historical commentaries, social diagnoses, or any display of erudition. He was writing in a much more sweeping dimension, placing man in a position of a universal dilemma which surpasses the bounds of his social or historical context. Nevertheless, we must ever bear in mind that his heroes and situations are in a very real sense not mere abstractions, but rather abstract depictions of very concrete people and their plight. Kafka's primary concern in his works is to expose the raw nerves of human experience to our scrutiny. The fact that he may do this by allegory, myth, symbols, or abstractions must never detract from the essential truth that he is dealing with the human situation. What he does, however, is tease our minds and imaginations beyond the boundaries of rationality, thereby plunging us into the supra-historical world of spiritual anxieties and metaphysical perplexities at once chilling, enthralling, and bewildering.

KAFKA, CAMUS, AND THE IDEA OF THE ABSURD

Camus' Essay on Kafka

In the appendix to his philosophical work, "The Myth of Sisyphus", Albert Camus has an essay entitled "Hope and the Absurd in the Work of Franz Kafka". Apart from its intrinsic merit as an example of Camus' thinking, it is worth examining from our point of view, inasmuch as it illuminates a certain amount of the profundity of Kafka's complex ideas. Camus starts by observing that the reader is forced to reread Kafka, since the absence of the normal type of ending in his works opens up the immediate possibility of several interpretations. We are warned that it is wrong to try to interpret all the details in the works of Kafka, principally because he is dealing in symbols. And when a writer writes in symbols, the reader must not approach his work with the intention merely of interpreting these symbols, since they express a form of reality beyond the comprehension of the writer himself. Camus points out, particularly with regard to *The Trial*, that it is often very difficult to discuss Kafka quite simply in terms of symbols, since a character like the accused, Joseph K., acts with a "naturalness" which baffles by its very simplicity. What is unique about Kafka's heroes is the simple way they react to extremely puzzling and paradoxical situations. Kafka's secret is in fact his subtle sense of ambiguity. In his works, there is an eternal tension between the ordinary and the extraordinary, in which logic and absurdity are apparently inextricably locked. In "The Metamorphosis", for example, there is an almost effortless lucidity in the reaction of the man to the beast he has become.

Camus stresses the fact that a perpetual dichotomy exists in Kafka: on the one hand, there is the everyday, or "natural" world, and on the other, there is the supernatural world of perplexities and anxiety. Kafka's works exemplify Nietzsche's dictum: "Great problems are in the street". The absurd in Kafka is expressed by a consistent translation of the particular into the general and vice versa, and by the very ordinariness of human reaction to abnormal events. The hero of "The Metamorphosis", for example, feels only a "slight annoyance" at having become a vermin. Yet Camus is very quick to point out the strange way in which hope is introduced into Kafka's works. He draws a distinct parallel between Kafka's thought and Kierkegaard's in this respect, inasmuch as the more tragic Kafka's heroes become, the fiercer is the hope. Camus sees *The Trial* as an absurd prelude to the impassioned and moving Kierkegaardian "leap" of *The Castle*. Kierkegaard in fact gave the perfect description of what is meant by hope in Kafka: "Earthly hope must be killed; only then can one be saved by true hope".

Kafka and the Absurd Hero

The hero as conceived by Kafka has been compared symbolically to Goethe's Werther and Byron's Manfred, inasmuch as he epitomizes for this century the alienation of man from his surroundings expressed in terms beyond the level of consciousness. Yet it should be pointed out that Kafka really did not owe any specific debt to past literary giants, nor did he lay the foundations of any tradition which has been emulated and improved upon. Kafka, in the depiction of his hero, captured the frightening elements of total despair which he himself experienced, and translated them into human dimensions against a background of myth, allegory, and spiritual longing. It would be wrong therefore to say that Camus follows "in the tradition of Kafka", but rather that his search took place in the same **metaphysical** territory.

There are of course striking similarities in their exploratory methods, for example, but these are strongly counterbalanced by the differences in their philosophical positions and destinations. Camus, for instance, sees Sisyphus as the symbol of the twentieth-century hero-using the word hero in its more traditional, "heroic", sense. Sisyphus, as Camus himself states, is stronger than the rock he is condemned to push. Camus' hero has a conscience which does not allow any guilt, an intellectual awareness which distinguishes him from an alien environment, a spiritual forcefulness which by its very existence does not allow anguish or despair to dominate. So the "absurd hero" of Camus cannot be equated with Kafka's central figures, who are tormented by fears and guilts in a nightmarish world of dark shadows and haunting memories. The futility of the struggle in Kafka is derived from the inner, subconscious fears and guilts which his heroes recognize but do not comprehend. But one cannot really talk of the "futility" of Sisyphus, who consciously defies and obliterates the hostile gods around him. There is a sense of elation in Sisyphus as he pushes the rock, and therein lies the hope of Camus, who was undoubtedly wrong in equating this with the hope in Kafka.

Kafka's hero does indeed struggle against alien gods - the law, the police, the authorities, and so on. But he does not comprehend why, since he is obsessed by an inner will totally beyond his understanding. There is an element of triumphant defiance in Camus' hero which is absent in Kafka's, whose hostile gods remain gods and remain hostile and whose heroes are heroes only inasmuch as they "hang on" in a state of bewilderment. Hope in Kafka does exist, and we recognize it, barely discernible as it is. But we don't know why it exists. Camus himself states that we must imagine that Sisyphus is happy. This is why his heroes are "absurd", in the sense that their defiance and scorn is absurd by his heroes' being conscious of them. Kafka's heroes are futile, because they continue the struggle conscious only of its futility and ambiguity. At a later point we will go into a more detailed analytical comparison of the works of Kafka and Camus.

HOW TO READ KAFKA

As we have already seen, Camus insisted that the very nature of Kafka's works demands that we read them twice. While this is certainly a valid statement, one may well be justified in pointing out that not many readers have the intellectual awareness or critical perceptions of a Camus. The question is immediately raised, therefore, of how one reads Kafka, since he is without doubt one of the most difficult authors to understand. Angel Flores, editor of a work called *The Kafka Problem*, claims that people who read Kafka-and even people who do not-all seem to end up with the conclusion not only that they know what he means, but also that only they know what he means. Interpretations of his works on a more scholarly level have led to astute and penetrating commentaries by sociologists, psychoanalysts, and theologians, all of whom claim with equal assurance to have special and definitive insights into Kafka's meaning.

We have already pointed out that Kafka's very obscurity is in itself an integral part of his total work, leaving open the possibility of many conflicting opinions. In this case, Kafka would have succeeded in stressing the obscurities, ambiguities, and perplexities of the human situation by showing the same qualities in his writings. Yet if Kafka is to be regarded as a major literary figure-which he is-his works must in themselves contain merits without the puzzling sub-strata of meanings which are the object of so much critical analysis. If a reader must have a thorough knowledge of Freud and the Talmud before he can appreciate Kafka, then Kafka cannot be considered a successful novelist per se. But he does succeed as a novelist, primarily because of the clarity with which he depicts the actuality of what is happening in his works, irrespective of the "sub-text". His consummate artistry as a writer asserts itself in such a way that his works can indeed be read and appreciated for their own intrinsic merits of style, narrative, and language.

Because of the plethora of analytical critiques which have sprung up around such works as *The Trial* and *The Castle*, for example, many readers approach these works primarily with the intention of unraveling the mysteries of their contents. Kafka should be read first and foremost for what he is actually saying, and appreciated for the language he uses in saying it. What he means by what he says may indeed prompt the reader to re-read and re-examine his works. But his works survive because Kafka was a great writer, not because he was a successful obscurantist.

INTERPRETATIONS OF KAFKA'S WORK

All the major commentators on Kafka are in accord on one point, namely, that there is a search involved in his works. Many claim that this search is purely of a religious nature. There is a wide disagreement, however, on what form the religious nature of the search takes. Some claim that Kafka's hero is engaged in an agonizing quest for the two gods, Justice and Grace, and that Kafka is therefore essentially writing about the nature of the Jewish cabala. Others have tried to prove that he is most decidedly Christian in his approach, and such critics point for verification to Kafka's affinity with the Christian Existentialist philosopher Kierkegaard. One commentator even sees close similarities between Kafka's thought and that of Karl Barth.

Although there is disagreement among adherents to this type of interpretation, it should be noted that any evaluation of Kafka from a religious point of view presupposes the fact that the ultimate goal of the hero is a good one. We can see, then, how one critic equated K.'s spiritual excursion in *The Castle* to that of Christian in *Pilgrim's Progress*-bearing in mind, of course, the profound difference in the conclusions of both journeys. This brings us again to the element of Kafka's hope which, as we noted, Camus stresses in "The Myth of Sisyphus". For even when the most pessimistic critics who approach Kafka from a religious standpoint see K.'s quest as an anguished longing for death, it is the death which brings with it the hope of eternal resurrection and salvation. From this angle, Kafka's works form one large allegory.

To counteract this critical position, it has been pointed out that Kafka's works-particularly *The Castle*-cannot possibly be regarded as a religious allegory in any way analogous to Bunyan's *Pilgrim's Progress*. Critics who adopt this attitude stress the fact that in a work such as *The Castle*, for example, there is no sense of pilgrimage, since there is no "motion" on the part of K., the central character, no sense of spiritual development or growth, no change. Nor does Kafka suggest that there is even the possibility of man's becoming a pilgrim in the religious sense of the word, or of his making even a semblance of progress.

The "anti-religious" school of Kafka criticism makes one major allowance, however: that Kafka's work concerns the religious longing of man, inasmuch as his heroes live in an age when spiritual values have been totally distorted or even annihilated. This school of critics aim their attack, therefore, not at Kafka's depiction of man's tormented position in a non-religious atmosphere, but rather at the critics of the "religious" school who assume that Kafka's-and K.'s-ultimate goal is God. The "anti-religious" critics would tend to make a statement such as this: "We agree that Kafka is a religious writer only in the sense that he depicts man as a pathetic, trapped creature struggling in a universe totally devoid of religious or spiritual values. Beyond that, however, we refuse to go, and we view the 'religious' interpretation of Kafka's works as symptomatic of the longing that lurks within the critics themselves. May we point out, however, that we do not necessarily agree with Kafka's statement of man's dilemma. Some of us even deplore the lack of more positive spiritual hope in Kafka's works. All we are saying is that critics who see K., for example, as a modern pilgrim are merely giving vent to their own deluded hopes. Such critics are merely refusing to believe what in fact Kafka is saying: man is the tortured, bewildered victim of a godless world devoid of hope or spiritual values".

Kafka and Man's Dilemma

At this point let us make a clear distinction. The critics we have just discussed are anti-religious in the sense that they do not interpret the Kafka hero in terms of man's spiritual longing. But in a very real way they sympathize with K., for example, and would certainly admit the meaningfulness of what Kafka is saying in the light of man's dilemma. There is yet another school of Kafka criticism, however, which would agree wholeheartedly with the first, "religious", school, in saying that Kafka is in fact a deeply mystical writer. They would further agree that a work such as *The Castle* is profoundly theological in nature and intent. But this admission on their part comes by way of scorn rather than praise, and their attack is concentrated not so much on Kafka's works or on any religious interpretation of his works as on Kafka himself.

They see Kafka almost as a psychopathic victim of sociological and historical circumstances, forced into a Kierkegaardian type of mediaeval mysticism because of his own personal inability to come to terms with any kind of sane reasoning. Kafka to them is a brilliant but intellectually perverted product of all that is tragic in German history, inasmuch as he was doomed to drift into his own private world of spiritual hallucination through a total inability to come to terms with the turmoil of German history or with any possible solutions to this turmoil. In sociological terms,

Kafka was a trapped man. He found existing society intolerable, he would have been horrified-and perhaps annihilated-by Hitler's answer for the doomed, and he would have seen nothing but spiritual torpidity in the ideals of democracy.

These critics-often referred to as the "naturalist" school-interpret the authority symbols in Kafka's works, which block any spiritual progress on the part of his heroes, as Kafka's own admission of his total inability to fit into society. Since, in their view, Kafka lived in the completely involuted nightmarish world of the psychopathic mystic, his works are but the manifestations of the desolated sense of doom which plunged him into death. In these critical circles, Sartre's famous dictum that "Hell is other people" would be paraphrased in Kafka-esque terms as: "Hell is myself and it is the State in which I am doomed to suffer".

An Approach to Reality

There is yet another school of critics who would agree with the above third group insofar as they would admit Kafka's awareness of the disastrous nature of such mysticism when placed in a totally alienated social context. But these critics regard Kafka as a supreme satirist, whose works are actually attacks on the type of mystical thinking which interprets the world entirely in terms of religious transcendentalism. They concede that Kafka himself found himself trapped - but trapped by a conscious, intellectual awareness that there are grave limitations to his (and man's) reasoning powers. Their claim is that Kafka, having recognized these limitations, was further aware that to fulfill himself completely, man must attempt to probe all possible ways of escaping from the confines of reason into the enriching world of spiritual values. But this quest is in fact a futile one, and what Kafka is really doing is making a detached, objective, and thoroughly rational observation on the pathetic, hopeless plight of man in his involved, subjective, and thoroughly irrational quest for an Ultimate which he can never possibly attain.

In these critical terms, therefore, the works of Kafka are really ironical fables, realistically conceived, in which he explores the desolate nature of this hopeless quest by the subtle but conscious use of Freudian symbols. One interpretation of *The Castle*, for example, is that the castle is really a mother symbol which K. is attempting to reach incestuously. This school of criticism is therefore saying, in fact, that Kafka fully recognizes man's plight, and indeed shares it. But Kafka's intellectual awareness and perceptive acumen is such that (a) he recognizes the hopelessness of seeking spiritual salvation beyond the frontiers of reason which enslave us all; (b) he is in a position to make a thoroughly detached and ironical commentary on this dilemma, and that (c) he believes that the basis for man's bewildered and frenetic search can in fact be explained in terms of Freudian psychology.

This interpretation of Kafka's works is admittedly an interesting one, but it tends to ignore certain statements regarding psychoanalysis which Kafka made elsewhere in his writings. In his *Contemplation*, for example, he refers to the "helpless error" of psychoanalysis. This school of criticism is in some ways the easiest to attack, inasmuch as it bases its analysis on the primary premise that Kafka makes no **allusions** to spiritual values in his novels. The obvious rejoinder that he makes no references to Freudian analysis, either, immediately opens up his works to any number of diverse interpretations.

Difficulties in Interpreting Kafka's Works

These are but a few of the critical approaches which at least point out not only that Kafka's works are the object of much controversial study, but - what is really more important - that they are most certainly worthy of examination and that they are brilliantly evocative. Now if one examines the above four schools of critical analysis carefully, it will be seen that these interpretations all bring to Kafka's works a part of their own particular creed, be it theological, atheistic, sociological, or psychoanalytical. They quite naturally read into a work like *The Castle* elements of their own particular philosophy, find in it remarkable parallels to their own thought and experience, and conclude that while other interpretations may be partly true, their insights into Kafka's meaning are obviously the only ones which are totally valid.

There is also the further temptation, to which so many people succumb, of building walls of academic and intellectual concepts around Kafka's works to such an extent that the works themselves become hidden from view. We have dealt very briefly, for example, with certain parallels and dissimilarities between Kafka and Camus, and we shall go into this comparison in more detail later. We have also touched on certain Kierkegaardian concepts found in Kafka. But let it be made quite clear that this is done, and should always be done, with the intention of casting light on many of the shadowy areas in Kafka's thinking. If this type of analysis is carried too far, literary criticism becomes a series of exercises in intellectual gymnastics. When we are dealing with a writer like Kafka, we must ever keep our focus concentrated on his own works, not on the works of writers in whom similar literary, philosophical, or theological concepts can be found.

Kafka's Approach to His Own Writings

While we shall be examining several interpretations of Kafka's major works, and in so doing draw on diverse aspects of their contents, the reader must in the long run read the works themselves and enjoy them for their own sakes. Only then can he pass his own judgment on whatever hidden meanings he may find in them. This brings us to the very important question of how Kafka himself approached the writing of his own works. In recent years a kind of Kafka cult has grown up which seems to presuppose that Kafka thought first and foremost in theological, philosophical, or allegorical terms, and decided to express the position he reached through the medium of fiction. It cannot be stressed too strongly that this is not the case, that Kafka was primarily a brilliant creative artist who thought in terms of images-a trial, a castle, a vermin-and, using that as his starting-off point, explored all the possibilities to which these images lent themselves.

In evaluations of Kafka's works, in short, too much stress can be laid on the underlying meaning, and not enough attention paid to the novel or the story itself. We must therefore take into consideration at all times the literary elements with which Kafka was primarily concerned as a writer-his images, the unity of his writing, the orchestration of his characterization and situations, the conflicts, and the coherence. It is not our purpose here to concentrate on one aspect of Kafka's writings alone, of course. We shall examine in some detail the various possibilities of meaning which lurk behind the ambiguities of the texts. But we must never forget that Kafka was neither a philosopher, a theologian, nor a psychoanalyst. He was a writer.

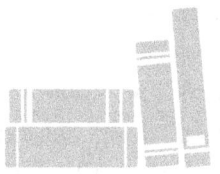

FRANZ KAFKA

SHORT WORKS

| BRIEF OUTLINE

Kafka's works consist of three major novels, *The Trial*, *The Castle*, and *Amerika*; collections of short stories, including "The Metamorphosis", "The Judgement", "In the Penal Colony", "A Country Doctor", and "The Great Wall of China"; and a variety of miscellaneous works, the most important of which are his *Parables*, *Diaries*, *Letters to Milena*, and "Letter to My Father". We shall proceed to examine the most important of these works in some detail, beginning with his stories and ending with the novels in which the main elements of his art and thought are to be found.

Kafka's writings really fall into two distinct periods, the first of which lasted until 1912, and the second of which extended for the next decade. As can be expected, the first period is marked by a sense of exploration, in which he sought original **themes** and a distinctive literary style. It is the period in which expressionism made its greatest impact on him, and which helped mold the artist who produced the great works of the second and final period. In his second period, Kafka's major works not only show the literary, philosophical, and spiritual influences of the first period, but are dominated to a great extent by the effect of his father on Kafka's personality. All of Kafka's works, however, have generally the unique qualities which make his writings thoroughly distinctive: the compact style, the dream-like mood, the seductively haunting atmosphere.

We shall now discuss briefly some of his minor works before examining in greater detail three of his most important works other than his novels; "The Metamorphosis", "A Country Doctor", and "In the Penal Colony".

DESCRIPTION OF A BATTLE

This is a novella, and is undoubtedly one of the most unsuccessful of all of Kafka's works. It is rather unwieldy constructed, and the **theme** of lonely frustration lacks the striking universality of tone which is the hallmark of his mature work. It makes interesting reading, however, inasmuch as it shows that Kafka was experimenting consciously with expressionism and surrealism, although unsuccessfully at this stage. He also tries to superimpose an element of the supernatural upon the dream world he creates, but, surprisingly enough, any success this novella enjoys comes from the beauty of his natural descriptions, including his use of symbols. On the whole, it is a more "open" work than the others, since there is an absence of the involuted tone of universal personalism which runs through his more mature works.

CONTEMPLATION

It is rather difficult to define or categorize this work. It consists of eighteen pieces which are not really stories, but rather a series of autobiographical notes or "contemplations" presented lyrically and dramatically. *Contemplation* first appeared in an edition limited to 800 copies, but immediately established his reputation among a small intellectual audience which recognized the talent contained in the slender volume. They have a poetically nostalgic air about them which does not appear often in Kafka's later works, but they nevertheless forecast the touches of **irony** which are always present even in his most advanced novels. One can also detect in this work a kind of plea, almost neurotic in nature, for the acceptance of the artist in society, and a tone of complaint against the staleness of the environment around him. This **theme** is particularly dominant in one of the pieces called "The Refusal" while his poetic qualities are shown to best advantage in one called "Children of the Highway".

It is particularly interesting to observe, when reading *Contemplation*, how Kafka has already begun-probably unconsciously-to indulge in a kind of dialogue with his own self, something worth bearing in mind when we come to analyze various aspects of his major works. In fact many of his great themes are in a sense presaged in this work: the illusory nature of the world, for example, is made evident in the few lines of the piece called "The Trees"; "The Runners" reveals his inability to make any bold decisions. Throughout these pieces also runs the strong element of struggle, in which forces like nostalgia and boredom seem to be pitted against desire and action. There is an emphasis on the use of symbols in *Contemplation*, many of which recur in his later works.

THE VERDICT

This is one of the most important of all of Kafka's minor works. In it are found most of the big **themes** which permeate his major writings, and although many of these are in embryonic form, they are nevertheless very definitely there. One of these, of course, is the conflict between father and son, set in a nightmarish atmosphere of stifling, dark symbols. Kafka himself was fascinated by the implications of this story, particularly by the relationship between father and son and the role of the friend as common link between them. His interpretation of his own story was roughly that Georg, the son, really possesses nothing, not even his fiancee, except through the friend—who serves as a common possession. Anything he has through the all consuming relationship with his father is automatically alien to him through the very fact of its being connected to his father.

Kafka viewed "The Verdict" as a clear picture of reality, but it has been suggested quite justifiably that he himself did not see the deep implications of his tale. There are many distortions in the story which, by the very fact of their appearing as reality, reveal the depths of Kafka's insights of which he himself was unaware. For example, the friend whom Kafka interprets as being the common denominator upon which Georg's relationship with his father is based, is in fact the symbol and source of all that keeps father and son apart. Kafka sees Georg as a human being whose void is filled up only by the image of his father, whereas the reality of the situation is that the father is himself a void, and that Georg's emptiness is an echo of the father's.

From a biographical point of view, "The Verdict" is particularly interesting because of the reverse roles which Kafka unconsciously depicts. For Georg is in fact an arrogant, pushing type of philistine whose traits are really those of Kafka's father, while the father in the story has all the spiritual, scrupulous sensitivities so characteristic of Kafka himself. The friend, on the other hand, who is seen by Kafka as a figure independent in identity from the father and son, is in fact a composite portrait of both. A failure, lonely, naive, a bachelor, he has all the traits of the real Kafka. On the other hand, he is forthright, a fighter, and has a strong, willful sense of independence-all characteristics of Kafka's father.

In *The Frozen Sea*, Charles Neider makes a fascinating interpretation of the psychological nuances inherent in this work. Kafka himself suffered lifelong guilt through his inability to emulate his father or satisfactorily fulfill the demands his father made on him. The pain was made even more intense by Kafka's own strenuous resistance to the very act of satisfying his father's wishes, an act which he considered would negate his own personality. In creating the portrait of Georg, therefore, Kafka is indulging in a form of self-flagellation by attributing to the son the qualities he hated in his own father. Kafka is thus obliterating his guilt by flailing himself for any elements of his father's personality which lurk within him. The friend, on the other hand, is really a symbol of the better side of Kafka's nature, the part openly challenged in the story by Georg's father. This is indicative of Kafka's feeling that his father was destroying the finer aspects of his character. Yet Georg's rejection of the friend also indicates Kafka's wish to obliterate these finer traits in order to ingratiate himself with his father.

THE HUNGER-ARTIST

The dominant mood of this work, which consists of several stories, the most important of which are "A Hunger-Artist", "First Sorrow", and "Josephine the Singer", is an **irony** tempered by a sense of peace. Since these stories were compiled into one short volume shortly before Kafka's death, they can probably be regarded as a **didactic** testimony to his own position as an artist, written with a certain detachment born of increasing maturity. We must not get the impression, however, that Kafka was here adopting the position of the artist's hero, defending his own feelings of failure and inadequacy on the grounds of alienation from a hostile and philistine society. On the contrary, there is a strong element in these stories of the artist's being satirized as well as explained.

The story called "A Hunger-Artist" is undoubtedly the best-known of the three, and more or less synthesizes Kafka's own role as the artist in society. In this tale, the hero reaches almost absurd heights of disastrous self-destruction in the interests of preserving and almost sanctifying his ego. Yet in line with what we have just said, Kafka does not merely extol his virtues by showing the artist as the embittered outcast or hapless victim of an unfeeling society. He is made to appear almost laughable, while at the same time is a thoroughly sympathetic figure. "First Sorrow", on the other hand, tends to concentrate on the loneliness and childishness of the artist in his desire to achieve perfection-in this instance as a trapeze artist.

"Josephine the Singer" views the artist from the point of view of the audience, and highlights his puzzling, enigmatic qualities. The fact that Kafka represents the artist as a mouse is an interesting comment alone on his own picture of himself. The artist in this story is depicted as a singer, none of whose musical qualities are recognized by the mouse world around it, but who is allowed to exist in society only by virtue of her overweening egotism. It would be safe to say that **irony** is the mood permeating this tale.

THE GREAT WALL OF CHINA

This work, also consisting of a series of stories, contains what are undoubtedly some of the best short pieces ever written by Kafka. Of these, the most powerful story is one called "The Married Couple", in which woman is depicted as having a power of spirit and a mental strength with which man-particularly within the marriage bond-cannot compete. Man in this story is depicted as a wreck; crippled not by physical disease, but by such qualities as his intellectual gifts and his ambitious drives. Kafka also introduces the interesting point here that man is overpowered by death, while woman conquers death by being unable to recognize it.

There are many very short stories in "The Great Wall of China" which are appealing not only for their intrinsic artistic merit, but also because of the techniques and virtuosity Kafka displays in them. One of these, called "A Common Confusion", uses letters instead of people, and introduces a comic element to demonstrate the confusion among human relationships. "Sancho Panza" is a delightful parable which serves as a slightly ironical commentary on the use of legend itself. "The Problem of Our Laws" is interesting from the point of view of Kafka's interest in social problems, which he discusses in terms of the clash between traditional classicism and the romanticism of youth.

Two outstanding stories in this work are "The Hunter Gracchus" and "The Bucket Rider". The first of these is a near-sardonic but fascinating commentary on death. By having the dead hunter Gracchus wander aimlessly about the earth after he has been killed, Kafka is in fact attempting to explode the myth that death is some kind of blessed release from the "mortal coils" of life. He suggests the frightening thesis that the poor outcasts of life should not necessarily seek solace in the possible refuge of a comforting and redeeming afterlife. Death, too, is a world in which there are outcasts who are equally bewildered by the meaninglessness of their trapped state. Yet Kafka somehow succeeds in making this situation not only absurd, but laughably absurd.

"The Bucket Rider" is a strange story, written in fantasy form, apparently to show that there is a cold, cruel steak in women which is absent in men, who at least have a conscience. Here, too, the effects of the First World War on social conditions show their influence on Kafka, since the story revolves around a man who is freezing to death through lack of coal.

MISCELLANEOUS AND FRAGMENTARY WORKS

The first of these is a novella which is probably one of the least successful of Kafka's minor works. He attempts here to make conscious, exploratory inroads into the haunting world of anxiety neurosis, but the end result is tiresomely labored and cumbersomely symbolic. One gets the impression on reading The Burrow, for example, that Kafka was being overintellectual in his attempts at inventiveness, and that somehow he negates his native creativity in so doing.

In "The Giant Mole", Kafka concentrates his attack on authority symbols-in this case in the world of science. The poet and critic Edwin Muir saw this work as representing an attack on the authority of science, but Charles Neider makes the subtle distinction that Kafka was criticizing scientific authorities, which is something a little different.

One of Kafka's most delightful and "humanly inhuman" works is one called "Blumfield, an Elderly Bachelor", which, although incomplete, reveals a quality of almost childlike fantasy. Although it is primarily a portrait of lonely bachelorhood-a **theme** well-known to Kafka-it is couched in such bizarre terms that the pathetic aspects of Blumfield's character are not swamped in gloom. The fact that the old bachelor becomes the object of possession by two bouncing balls is in itself a startling idea, and Kafka uses it with most appealing effect. Note the subtle, paradoxical symbolism used here, however. Blumfield, the elderly bachelor, would appear to be simply an object of our pity, lightened somehow by amusement untainted with scorn. Kafka makes us accept this, then proceeds to examine the dimensions of the situation with merciless wit and ruthless **irony**. For the implication is made throughout all his doddering eccentricities, and for all the sadness implicit in his elderly bachelorhood, Blumfield is a selfish parasite. He is also an outcast, inasmuch as he has lived his way into being "different" from society. In the course of this process, he has become virtually "inhuman". And by attributing to bouncing balls "human" parasitic qualities, and by having them possess Blumfield, Kafka is making a supremely ironical commentary on the paradoxical dilemmas inherent in social loneliness.

Many of Kafka's shorter pieces were published posthumously, and most of them-including "The Denial", "The Helmsman", and "The Examination"-contain elements of the **themes** that dominate his major works, namely, the bewildering and paradoxical aspects of human existence which cancel each other out, leaving men struggling on and on in isolation and guilt. A few-such as "In Our Synagogue", and "A Guest Among the Dead", have explicit Jewish themes.

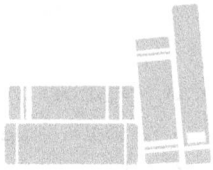

FRANZ KAFKA

THE METAMORPHOSIS

....

This is not the only one of Kafka's works dealing with animals; in "Josephine the Singer", for example, he deals with a mouse, and in "A Report to an Academy" we have an ape as the central figure. In "The Metamorphosis", however, Kafka's approach is different from that which he takes with others, inasmuch as the main character, a commercial traveler called Gregor Samsa, has assumed the form and the propensities of a huge vermin. In the other two stories, the animals have adopted the characteristics and qualities of humans. It is interesting also to note that the opening sentence of "The Metamorphosis", telling us of the appalling transformation, is in fact the end of Gregor's ordeal. The reader's interest is immediately focused simultaneously in two directions by the opening sentence, since he wants to know how the creature is going to adjust to and react to humans in the future, and is also fascinated by the reasons for his having been transformed into an insect in the first place. The implication is also there that Gregor has been punished for some crime or other, and that the opening of the story is in one way the end of a tale of crime, punishment, and guilt. Yet Kafka very cleverly never openly puts the question to us as to why the transformation actually took place. The reader is therefore in the position of simply having to accept the fact of its having taken place, and of following the narrator as he flits from the "realistic" world of humans and the "surrealistic" world of beasts. Yet the question of Gregor's guilt remains, for he is in a very special sense a prisoner who has been captured by some authority or other; but the nature of his guilt has to be captured in turn by the reader. We shall see later how the reader is placed in a similar position when confronted by the plight of Joseph K. in *The Trial*.

There are many disturbing aspects of this story, particularly if Kafka intended it to be regarded as an autobiographical allegory. For Gregor, by his very metamorphosis, is in a position of automatic alienation to his environment, and his relationship with the human world is one of outsider versus opponents. It is equally disturbing to note that Gregor Samsa does not resemble a vermin-he is one. The sense of fascination and horror one receives at the opening of the story is heightened by Gregor's reaction to the discovery of his transformation. A frightening suggestion of rational acceptance is established, with a concomitant mood of submission to the verdict that has been delivered and to the punishment that has been meted out.

There are three distinct sections in this story, each one of which we will examine in detail: Gregor Samsa's relation to his job, his family, and himself. His ultimate fate comes as a kind of synthesis intended to unify the three facets of Gregor's relationships.

GREGOR AND HIS JOB

Time plays a very important part in the first section of "The Metamorphosis". The traveling salesman's awareness of the change that has taken place coincides with the deadly and inexorable sense of time passing. Note how Kafka imposes upon the reader an almost desperate sense of inhuman, mechanized urgency by constantly reminding us of the time. The suggestion has been made that Gregor willed, or more precisely "dreamed" his way into an insect, almost by way of preferring his new fate to that of a mechanized salesman. At this point, however, we must bear in mind that Kafka has, in another context, made Gregor the very human victim of an inhuman act of his parents. Before the metamorphosis took place, therefore, Gregor was the trapped victim of a ruthless social situation created by lust for money.

An interesting and very subtle historical situation is highlighted here. The manager's personal relationship with Gregor's family is indicative of the more relaxed "Old World" type of system under which economic deals could be and were made on a human level. Yet, as we have seen, Gregor has not only become the hapless end product of such a relationship, but has also been catapulted into the soul-destroying impersonality of the "new world" organizational set up. This is why Kafka, by physically positioning his characters in a particular way, gives the suggestion of proximity and distance simultaneously. Gregor is obviously bound and beholden to authority, but is at the same time totally isolated from it.

Kafka makes the brilliant point that his hero does not want his freedom, while at the same time he craves it. The gateway to his freedom lies open before him, but as he approaches it he shies away from it. His dual awareness of this possibility and of the impossibility of his acting upon it, the longing for liberty and his dread of it, have placed him in an intolerable situation which he somehow tolerates. Gregor's speech to the General Manager is brilliantly written, the lost cry of a vermin with nothing to offer but its own repulsive self. It is important to note that Gregor's acceptance of the metamorphosis, coupled with his fascination with his own words, has made him virtually forget his new state.

Comment

We mentioned earlier the possibility of Gregor's having willed his own way into the world of vermin. But this would surely imply that he desired some kind of escape from the realistic world of enslaved salesmanship into the surrealistic world of the liberated vermin. In view of what happened after the arrival of the General Manager, however, this is not a totally plausible explanation. Gregor not only accepts the transformation that has taken place, but also demonstrates a desperate need to remain in the trapped world of commercialism which he also loathes. His desperate pleadings constitute one of the most poignant parts of Kafka's writings, and is eloquent testimony to man's frenetic and futile attempt to escape from himself by pleading to remain as he is. Kafka makes his plight excruciating and intolerable by desperately inexorable windings of time and movement.

GREGOR AND HIS FAMILY

In the second phase of the story, Kafka concentrates a great deal on time, which has both moved and been suspended. Kafka employs the brilliant technique here of deliberately confusing the reader as to the time lapse which has taken place. We know that it is twilight, but it is a twilight that is vaguely defined and amorphous, in marked contrast to the overabundant details of the ticking seconds at the beginning of the story. We feel, therefore, that this twilight is in a sense the dawn of a new phase in Gregor's relationships with the society around him; and the branch of society here is his own family.

Kafka gives us a terrifying portrait of the malaise which has engulfed his hero, and concentrates on the sense of Gregor's imprisonment. It is almost as if Kafka is talking of man's being doubly incarcerated by society and by his own nature. The mood of impending doom is intensified by Kafka's use of light in this passage. Few passages in literature can equal this description of total, terrifying solitude.

Comment

At this point Kafka very brilliantly moves into a new dimension of human relationships with regard to Gregor's family. Having established the fact of Gregor's resigned acceptance of the change, and having stressed the resultant sense of diseased isolation, Kafka makes us realize that the adjustment to the situation must now come from Gregor's family, not from Gregor. His tentative introductions to the character of Gregor's family takes the place of the sounds of their voices. Note, too, how the mother's identity gradually melts into a kind of anonymity. Here again, Kafka introduces the element of dichotomous proximity and distance expressed in terms of familial alienation. There is obviously a strong autobiographical element here as well, since Kafka elsewhere in his writings expressed the opinion that his mother abdicated her positive position as his mother for a negative role in the shadow of his father. With regard to Gregor's father, it is important to note that Kafka does not overstress the portrayal, since the metamorphosis in itself creates enough of a gulf between father and son without accentuating paternal idiosyncrasies. What Kafka does do, however, is give an ideal portrait of the bourgeois type father of his era: patriarchal in attitude, human in his assertive pig-headedness, natural in the temporary rejuvenation resulting from the obligation placed upon him. In other words, Kafka makes the father's reactions thoroughly credible and natural, whereas any overreaction on his part would have been an unnecessary commentary on the horror of Gregor's position.

Here Kafka introduces an ironical aspect of the circumstances which led to the transformation, and which makes us aware of an ingrained weakness and submissiveness in the father, which further explains the same traits in Gregor. Kafka depicts here the almost parasitic nature of two weaknesses in characters who in fact feed off each other's failings.

The family member on whom Kafka concentrates most, however, is Gregor's sister, Grete. She is the only one who comes to terms with the transformation in as humane a way as possible. One of the most interesting aspects of this part is the diverse reactions on the part of the family to the furniture in Gregor's room. In some ways this is one of the most crucial parts of the whole story, since the question of Gregor's identity revolves around his decision in relation to their attitude. Kafka very cleverly implies that Gregor is still Gregor the salesman, but shows us that what he really sells now is any claim to that identity by acquiescing to Grete's wishes. As soon as he does this he waives any claim to his own transmogrified personality and surrenders to the fact that he is an insect who has replaced Gregor.

THE PROBLEM OF GREGOR'S IDENTITY IN PART TWO

Kafka does not resolve the identity problem quite as neatly as this, however. One of the dominant **themes** in Kafka is this very question of identity; insoluble, perhaps, but one which creates many of the bewildering paradoxes and ambiguities throughout his works. For Gregor's struggle is not just a question of his inability to relate to society around him, but his inability to relate to his self, mainly because he does not know the nature of his self. We shall find this problem arising more intensely in works like *The Trial* and *The Castle*. Now Gregor's fight to cling to his identity is depicted in the powerful, moving passage in which he covers the print of the woman with the fur stole. Since this print, which is covered with glass, was one of his proudest possessions, his attempt to hold on to it and protect it by crawling over it-almost by way of comforting it-is poignantly symbolic. For Gregor-like Kafka-had been a confirmed and, presumably, lonely bachelor who had lavished a great deal of love on the print. As the insect presses its body against the glass, however, we realize the futility and hopelessness of such attempted love and possession. Although the object of Gregor's hopeless infatuation is just a cheap print, he cannot ever possess it completely - for the glass is always between them. Here again we have the recurring Kafka **theme** of nearness and distance, a sense of the irrevocable loss that comes from unbearable closeness.

The bizarre and almost ludicrous ending is symbolic from many points of view. Even the end of the insect's existence is marked by bewilderment and tormented confusion.

Comment

The implication has been made that Kafka was making deliberate reference to the Tree in the Garden of Eden, by the father's use of apples, with all the conscious, concomitant implications of sin and the loss of love. Here we must be careful not to read too much into the work, although it is more than probable that Kafka is making deliberately ambiguous allegorical references throughout "The Metamorphosis" to heighten the general atmosphere of tension and mystery. For it is very important to note that Kafka does not provide any answers in this story. Nor, for that matter, does he deliberately raise any questions. What he does is turn our attention in many directions at once, using a variety of conflicting images, and in so doing opens our eyes to the puzzling and often unanswerable problems of human existence.

GREGOR AND HIS SELF

The whole question of reconciling himself, not only to his family and environment, but also to his "self", is one which besets Gregor, not so much through a growing process of intellectual awareness as through the impact made on him from without, particularly with regard to his relationship with his sister. At this juncture it should be made clear that there was some hint of an incestuous desire on Kafka's part toward his own sister, Valli. If aspects of "The Metamorphosis" are indeed to be regarded as autobiographical, Gregor's relationship to his sister and the effect which her change had on him would suggest that this was possibly so. Kafka has been criticized for this "switch" in Grete's attitude, inasmuch as it seems a move contrived by him to make Gregor's dereliction and utter prostration more desolate. At the end, Kafka does not even allow Gregor the luxury of morbid introspection. Kafka may well be taken to task here for "overloading" Gregor's plight to some degree.

Against this, one can cite the strange and moving passage, one of the most revealing and moving **episodes** in the story where Gregor responds to his sister's playing the violin in a very human and civilized way, which suggests that he is a human with the form of a vermin. But Gregor the human being, Gregor the traveling salesman, was not emotionally stirred by beautiful music. This leads us to the possible conclusion that only by undergoing a process of metamorphosis, only by becoming a totally alienated creature, divorced from the crass banalities of human existence, could Gregor become his true self. This may well be Kafka's way of saying that total commitment to one's true identity would involve an act of utter rebellion against a society determined to negate such an identity. And such an act of rebellion would correspondingly carry with it such punishment and guilt that it would in fact constitute a form of suicide.

Kafka gives the reader the feeling of Gregor's overwhelming guilt, and it is centered somehow on his attitude to music. The reader is still faced with the nature of Gregor's guilt, which in some way led to his being transformed in the first place. Why, for example, does Kafka speak of the nourishment the insect craves as being unknown? What is the nature of this nourishment? From the context in which it is used, it would seem that music is the nourishment referred to, and this music may be, in Shakespeare's words, "the food of love" - which Gregor has been denied, or rather which he has refused to allow himself to receive.

One could go on and on, of course, speculating on the reasons for and nature of Gregor's guilt, and more often than not find oneself up against an impasse. The only reality of which we can be sure is that Gregor's metamorphosis took place as some form of punishment inextricably bound with all-consuming guilt. This guilt manifests itself in ever-encircling paradoxes and ambiguities which not only cannot be answered, but which are perhaps intended by Kafka to be answers in themselves.

Comment

It is important to note with regard to what we said earlier about Camus, Kafka, and the "hero" concept, that Gregor's life and death has not in any manner been heroic in the classical sense. Unlike Sisyphus, he displayed no sense of joyous revolt which could raise him in any way above the obstacles constituting his penance. Gregor's posture was one of submissiveness. He perhaps had an opportunity to indulge in the kind of introspection that might conceivably have led to some measure of self-knowledge. Instead of that, however, he turned outward to cling to anything tangible that might relate him to his real self. But his efforts are in vain. We have the frightening impression not that he has been drained of life, but that there was no real life there to begin with.

The really chilling thing about the image of Gregor as presented to us by Kafka is that his desperate attempts to cling to his identity are totally futile, since he had no real identity to begin with. The only "real" thing that Gregor can cling to is his consuming sense of guilt. But there is no ostensible reason for his feeling guilty, which automatically obliterates the possibility of atonement. Gregor is therefore in the position of having to accept his punishment, and the reader is in the concomitant position of having to accept Gregor's submissiveness.

THE METAMORPHOSIS: A SUMMING UP

Readers are often puzzled by the strange fascination which this story holds for them. It goes beyond the realm of being a successfully narrated tale of the macabre. The reason probably lies in the fact that Kafka has done something quite remarkable as a writer, inasmuch as he has taken an incident which lies in the imaginary world beyond reality and brought it back into the world of reality. The reader, in fact, becomes the insect. Another remarkable factor about the story is that Gregor has never been a person of great social importance, nor have his sins been of the magnitude that would warrant such a frightful punishment. There is obviously no great social message here, since no descent from nobility to abjectness is inherent in the tale. There is no unhappy beginning and happy ending to this story - nor is there a happy beginning and tragic ending. From start to finish it is in one way a drama of weakness, guilt, and abjectness.

Another interesting thing to note about "The Metamorphosis" is the absence of a supernatural outside force controlling the situation. No deus ex machina descends into the Samsa house. What happens with an inexorable, inviolable incomprehensibility which the reader is forced to accept-and which, by its very perplexity, makes it one of the most enthralling stories ever written. In many ways it is a tale of total negation written so positively that the abhorrent unreality of its contents becomes a fascinating reality. Kafka has made the impossible seem possible. It is a frightening thought that while Kafka leaves much unexplained in this story, some of the answers are provided by many of its readers who find an almost unbearable sense of identification with the traveling salesman, his family, and the insect he becomes.

The epilogue to the story seems somehow out of place. The images of sunshine, warmth, and good health do not seem a real part of Kafka's art which, terrible as it may sound, is more at home in the dark shadows of a crawling insect totally alienated from all around it.

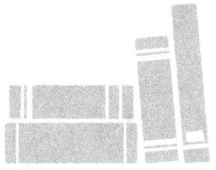

FRANZ KAFKA

A COUNTRY DOCTOR

This collection of stories was published in 1919, as was "In the Penal Colony", which we will be discussing shortly. By the time he came to write these works, Kafka had matured enough artistically and intellectually to be able to employ a device like the parable to reveal the reality behind the "real" world of empirical evidence. Before we examine the contents of "A Country Doctor" and all their implications, however, it is necessary to look at the parable as it has been used traditionally. We shall then be able to see the degree to which Kafka refined it as an art form worthy of expressing the religious doubts and **metaphysical** cravings which he himself experienced.

THE PARABLE IN LITERATURE

We must remember that in a very special sense Kafka is a writer of crisis, particularly of the religious crisis which besets twentieth-century man when the concept of "God" is one which cannot be expressed in the simplistic terms which were more satisfying, intellectually, in earlier ages. But Kafka is not to be regarded as a modern, revolutionary precursor of the parable as an attempted means of voicing modern man's dilemma. He belongs, in fact, to a tradition found in Heine and Nietzsche in the nineteenth century, although Kafka is unique in having perfected such parabolic usage. Heine himself saw the tremendous potential of the parable, and Nietzsche translated this potential into actuality, particularly by the striking use of the madman in *Joyful Wisdom*. The crazed man who screams through the marketplace looking for God among the very people who have destroyed God, is in fact a nihilistic type of modern Diogenes who has somehow or other strayed into a modern Biblical parable set in terms of **irony**. In the Bible, the parable was used as a device to illuminate an ultimate truth to be believed implicitly and to be lived explicitly. In Kafka, however, no such clear-cut religious context exists, and the activity involved in the paradox is the frenetic expression of a **metaphysical** longing which exists outside the precise abstractions of Biblical truths. Quite literally, there is a "fantastic" element in all modern parables-Dostoevsky's Grand Inquisitor being a prime example - but this element is consciously essential by the very nature of the problems which elicited the parable. In its Biblical **connotation**, the parable was used most effectively to bridge a gap between the unknown and the knowable, and to help the lonely wanderer cross that bridge. In its modern usage, however, exemplified at its best in Kafka, the parable is used to expose to us not only that the gap is there, but that man is totally ignorant of why it is there and that he finds himself in the insoluble dilemma of being unable to bridge, close, or comprehend the gap. Kafka's parables are expressions of his own sense of perpetual inadequacy, futility and almost unbearable longing.

THE TITLE STORY

It is somewhat surprising that Kafka chose the story called "A Country Doctor" as the title of the complete work, since its content is so difficult as to be almost inexplicable. Added to this difficulty is the fact that Kafka had not really mastered the technique of writing such a story, and the same criticism can be leveled against several of the tales in this collection. Yet there is a savage beauty inherent in the story which undoubtedly springs from its visionary quality, its pace, and the atmosphere of compelling horror.

Comment

As a story in itself, its main value would appear to be a purely biographical one, inasmuch as it exposes the turmoil of Kafka's mind at the time of its composition. Its lack of orchestration and thematic unity nevertheless suggest that the writer did not lose control of his subject matter, but that he did not have a clearly defined subject matter to begin with. From the structural point of view alone, it is uneven and halting, which could be assets, of course, if handled with studied control. In this case, the fragmentary, halting effects merely succeed in intensifying the overall opaqueness.

What then, are the possible reasons for Kafka's having chosen this as his title story? Several explanations have been put forward, each one of which have a certain validity. The story does contain several bold, chilling strokes, such as the very fact that the hero is a totally helpless creature whose job it is to help other people - the kind of paradoxical human situation so common in Kafka's works. Another explanation is that Kafka - who dedicated the book to his father - is making some kind of statement here on the father-son relationship which tortured him throughout his life. The bond between doctor and patient and the hopeless gulf existing between them could well be interpreted as a depiction of the situation which existed between

Kafka and his own father. Perhaps the most sound explanation lies in the portrait of the country doctor himself, who, clothed in the nakedness of dehumanized isolation, personifies so much of the human plight that is central to Kafka's themes.

ANIMAL IMAGES IN A COUNTRY DOCTOR

This concept of dehumanized isolation in Kafka often finds expression in his use of animals. As we have already seen, Gregor Samsa's transformation into an insect at once establishes the idea of a subhuman creature unsure of its identity-certain of its bestial nature and puzzled by its human qualities. Kafka seems to be at his most brilliant when dealing with this kind of image, and the stories contained in "A Country Doctor" have many examples of this device. In "Jackals and Arabs" for example, we have jackals who use language with devastatingly ironic effect. "The New Advocate" gives us the portrait of a battle charger who has turned into an advocate, while in "A Report to an Academy" we have an eloquent ape commenting on the human situation. Perhaps the most frightening use of the animal image is found in "An Old Manuscript Page" in which the nomads not only talk in the language of jackdaws, but have also assumed the characteristics of the horses they use. Note, too, the uncanny way in which Kafka creates the stench of death around these "non-human humans" who prowl the earth like scavengers of the dead.

It is interesting to study Kafka's use of animals in juxtaposition to the traditional use of animals in fables. One naturally expects a message of some kind in such an art form, but the message in Kafka's case lies not so much behind, as in, the use of animals and their relationship with human beings. With Kafka, there is always the baffling question of the identity of the creatures depicted. Are they animals or human beings? Are they human beings who have assumed the traits of animals? Are they animals who have adopted human propensities? These questions often remain unanswered, and deliberately so.

Comment

Often Kafka gives the impression that the freedom and innocence associated with animal life is infinitely preferable to the trapped guilt of humanity, and this point of view seems to be exemplified in "A Report to an Academy".

DEHUMANIZATION IN A COUNTRY DOCTOR

It should be pointed out that this process of **dehumanization** which permeates the stories in "A Country Doctor" does not only find expression in animal-human transference. In other stories dealing primarily with human beings, Kafka concentrates on their inhuman attributes.

Some rather overworked explanations have been offered toward Kafka's meaning in "A Fratricide", one of which suggests that Schmar represents Jewish bachelorhood-and therefore Kafka himself-and that the tale is Kafka's revolt against the celibate state he loathed. The answer undoubtedly lies in the very inhumanness of the deed. No sense of the traditional "reverence for life" is found in this story. The characters are puppets, acting rigidly with no feelings, no motivation, and no thoughts.

The same type of atmosphere is created in another story called "Up in the Gallery", which centers on a circus equestrienne.

Kafka also captures the same soulless, ritualistic atmosphere of the whole performance, and of the audience's reaction. Kafka here is revealing the unbearable pain which man feels when he actually becomes aware of the mechanized, soulless ritual of life around him.

This central idea is taken one step further in two strange stories: "A Visit to a Mine" and "Eleven Sons". There is a link between the stories in the "riddle" of the sons and engineers, the key to which is held by the servant and the father. We are never told the answer to the mystery, for although we are told details about the sons and engineers, the only clear fact that emerges is that the father and the servant both possess all the traits of the other characters. Kafka very cleverly individualizes each of the characters in the two groups, but as he does so their characteristics merge into one another to give an overall blurred effect. The only people who stand out in any way at all as individuals are the servant and the father, who both end up as enigmas merely reflecting the other shadowy personalities.

Comment

There are obviously strong autobiographical elements in the symbols of these stories-job and family being predominant, as they are in "The Metamorphosis". There have been various interpretations of the meaning of the numbers eleven and twelve that further link stories. The most plausible of these theories is that the twelfth figure represents the end of the time cycle on a clock, at which point the endless, timeless, ticking process begins over again. Note here the further resemblance to the opening of "The Metamorphosis", representing the ruthless, inexorable demands made by the passing of time. This frightening concept of time is the central destructive force in another story called

"The Next Village", in which a grandfather's reflections on time turn him into a kind of lifeless plant.

THE EXTRAHUMAN ELEMENT IN A COUNTRY DOCTOR

Up to this point, we have discussed stories which in some way or other reflect the human situation in human or inhuman terms. Human beings are represented as beasts, or vice versa; or they are depicted as machine-like puppets; or, when they are revealed as human beings, they are shrouded in strange, paradoxical mists. There is one story, however, called "The Worries of a Family Man", in which a "thing" appears which has no apparent relation to the human sphere at all.

Kafka's description of the thing is deliberately absurd, full of ludicrous technical jargon obviously intended as a jibing commentary on the mechanical aspects of twentieth-century existence. Odradek is a strange creature, even for a "thing" from some extra-human dimension. It is fanciful and even amusing- perhaps even absurd - but the family man is quick to note that it is somehow or other perfect. One can only hazard a guess at Kafka's meaning here: perhaps he is throwing up his hands at any possibility of perfection on a human level, or he may even be saying that perfection is recognizable from a human posture, but that its appearance is totally absurd. Neither of these explanations is completely valid, however, since Odradek has an alien or even forbidding quality about it which seems to imply some kind of warning to the family man. And in a sense Odradek is made very real - more real than the family man, in fact. It is not a living creature, yet we are told that it cannot die. Odradek also suggests by its presence that the unreality whence it came is fantastically close to the reality of the human sphere.

Comment

What then, does Kafka mean by it all? According to Kafka, the realm occupied by humans is being continually invaded, as it were, by Odradeks who are messengers from a realm beyond our comprehension. But our human realm is in fact a dehumanized one, and the realm beyond this - the one man calls "divine" - is in fact devoid of divinity. That is why Odradek is just a name who is perfect but unknowable, a messenger with no message, a "thing" that appears as a kind of cosmic reminder that bewildering chaos reigns among us.

To put it in almost absurd terms, it is as if a fragment of God had broken off at the moment of God's death, and lingers behind as a mere word to remind the family man that God is dead, that **dehumanization** is all around, and that the very appearance of Odradek, the perfect "thing", is proof of man's chaotic state. Perhaps the most frightening thought of all is that the family man is aware of the prohibitive nature of Odradek's presence- meaning that to cling to any God concept is not only inadvisable, but virtually forbidden. God's fleeting, fragmentary appearance brings not peace but terror, not solace but infinite loneliness.

FRANZ KAFKA

IN THE PENAL COLONY

....

Written in 1914 and published in 1919, "In the Penal Colony" is the longest of all Kafka's short stories. It is particularly interesting to study it in relation to the **theme** of dual reality we have just discussed, for in it Kafka ventures tentatively into the **metaphysical** world of the Divine which fascinated and terrified him. Here again we have a "thing" as we had in "The Worries of a Family Man (Odradek)", which stands not only at the center of Kafka's story, but also obviously at the center of his thinking. In this case it is a machine, an apparatus that dominates the story and dwarfs the characters into nameless nonentities by comparison.

THE NATURE OF THE MACHINE

The machine, by its very setting in a bleak penal colony, symbolizes at once the ruthless execution of the captors' power and the inescapable fate of the prisoners. Kafka creates certain paradoxes around the machine which have a meaning in themselves. The machine has a vicious function to perform - the unspeakable torture of the living. Even the nature of the torture is symbolic of much in Kafka's thinking. Man suffers by feeling guilt, but suffers even more by having the details of his guilt carved onto his very being.

Comment

The callousness with which Kafka tells his story is indicative of the writer's indifference to the importance of physical suffering. One almost senses a terrifying joy in Kafka himself as he describes the suffering. There is also a feeling of near-demonic triumph as he speaks of the spectators.

THE PURPOSE OF THE MACHINE

At first glance, the purpose of the machine seems as simple as its mechanism. But Kafka's machine has the unique purpose of punishing prisoners while making them aware of their crimes, yet it neither gives the culprit a chance to repent, nor does it prevent other people from committing similar crimes. To Kafka, the excruciating pain of the process is of minimal importance. It has been suggested that Odradek and the machine are both messengers from a world of reality beyond our comprehension. Note also that they are both described most realistically.

Comment

Another question that springs to mind in relation to the purpose of the machine is the nature of the law which promulgates and sponsors such a punishment. At first glance, who would say that such a law is obviously a perverted figment of Kafka's warped imagination, and that it could not possibly exist in civilization as we know it. Yet one cursory glance at some of the major events of twentieth-century history suggests that meaningless, vicious, and lethal laws are more than possible. Ironically enough, Kafka's machine seems more just than the hideous machines of totalitarianism which have operated within living memory. At least Kafka's condemned have a meaningful revelation, an apparently logical explanation for the illogical suffering they are enduring. The problem of the nature of the law involved - a problem we will be examining in some detail in *The Trial* - leads naturally to the question of the guilt which prompted the execution of the punishment.

THE QUESTION OF GUILT

There is a peculiar simplicity and lack of confusion regarding the guilt suffered by the victim. The ritualistic uselessness of his routine life is again symptomatic of Kafka's ideas on the malaise that blights humanity; and his rebellion, invoked by fatigue, is the paradoxical one of threatening the Captain with extinction. Yet Kafka very cleverly avoids the trap of having the Captain show any human emotion.

Comment

The important point made here-and one which, as we shall see, is reiterated in *The Trial*-is that there is absolutely no question of the man's guilt; again a testimony to Kafka's recurring **theme** of the inevitability of guilt. Kafka seems to be saying that while humanity en masse suffers guilt and is punished in the same way for this guilt, the nature of the crime is highly personal and individual. The law is universal, but the pain of punishment is suffered according to the precise details each human being's guilt.

KAFKA'S USE OF DOUBT

When we come to study *The Trial*, we shall see that the accused, Joseph K., doubts the legal code which is persecuting him. In this story, however, the victim is intellectually incapable of doubting anything, and to fulfill this function Kafka introduces a strange character called the Explorer. This character has been interpreted as representing Kafka himself, or rather Kafka's doubts about the validity and justice of guilt feelings. This could be a valid point, but on the other hand, one could just as readily identify Kafka's position with that of the prisoner or even the officer.

The Explorer-who is the major Doubt symbol of the story-is a strange, nameless figure Kafka is obviously suggesting here the necessity of complete distance from the human dilemma if any impartial judgment is to be made. The Explorer also seems to symbolize justice in its most civilized humanitarian sense. It would seem, then, that the doubt expressed by the visitor has directly caused the total collapse of the legal system under which the colony has been operating and that, in the traditional sense, justice has been done. From what we have already seen of Kafka's thinking, however, such a simple answer is highly improbable. Perhaps a closer examination of some detailed aspects of the story will reveal the more complex ideas inherent in the story.

THE MACHINE

Three possible associations come to mind when we consider what Kafka meant by the machine: that it represents man's self-destructive penchant for **dehumanization**; that it symbolizes the mysterious legal process we shall study later in the *The Trial*; or that it is a manifestation of modern barbarous technology under the aegis of some divinely ordained martial law. It could also be an image of the lethal quality of writing, made more fascinating by the labyrinth of lines which constitute the Designer's instructions. This may well be Kafka's commentary on the esoteric characteristics of his own particular art form. The officer, on the other hand, believes what he sees as representing reality. The duality of these two positions, the Designer's and the officer's, is in some ways symptomatic of Kafka's art.

Comment

While the script itself gives a clear message, it is nevertheless one which points to a realm beyond reality. The word "script" also has a Biblical **connotation** here (Scripture) and Kafka is obviously associating religious belief as expressed in the written word with a torture machine. Yet he does not do this as a cheap condemnation of traditional religion, but rather as an expression of the cruel process necessary before spiritual freedom can be attained. The spiritual freedom which Kafka craved consisted of freedom from the body and the reality it implies. There is also a paradoxical aspect to Kafka's use of the script and the torture machine as religious symbols, inasmuch as they negate the injunction, "Thou shalt not kill". Moreover, these symbols have a universal character to them, being indicative of the belief - which we shall discuss later in relation to Kierkegaard and *The Castle* - that man has not killed God, but rather that God can make inhuman demands on man to the extent of killing him.

THE NEW COMMANDANT

Our immediate impression of the new Commandant is one of moderation. Kafka very subtly implies, however, that the new order may well be marked by an effete type of weakness as a result, and that the efficiency of the colony may conceivably suffer. There is a strong implication here of Kafka's using Woman as the symbol of temptation, the historical cause of man's downfall. We are left with the impression that while the old regime as promulgated by the former Commandant was dictatorial and unjust, the new era may well be one marked by corruption and dissolution.

THE EXPLORER

It would be wrong to regard the Explorer as a symbol of modern enlightened civilization embodying all the best humanitarian attributes of our age. He has been described more accurately as a "practicing cultural relativist", whose initial hostility toward the machine represents an almost haughty attitude toward a culture inferior to his own. He represents the indifferent, almost cynical attitude of modern man brutalized by so-called "technological advances", and we are left with the feeling that he has been unaffected by what he has experienced.

THE PENAL COLONY

Although Kafka typically does not give any clearly defined answers to the future he expects, or intends, for his Penal Colony, he gives some implications of what might conceivably happen.

Comment

The teahouse seems to be a sanctuary or a shrine. There is evangelical ring about the scene, which may well be Kafka's way of depicting Judaism resurrected in the form of Christianity, with a Christ-like sacrificial act on a mechanized version of the Cross. Yet this explanation does not prove completely satisfactory. What then, will the Second Coming bring? In Yeat's phrase, "What rough beast slouches toward Bethlehem to be born?" Kafka leaves us pondering, as he does so often, in an ambivalent mood of fear and awesome expectancy.

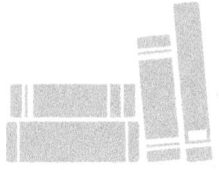

FRANZ KAFKA

THE TRIAL

GENERAL COMMENTS

As a novel, *The Trial* shows a structural unity and stylistic mastery which makes it one of Kafka's more mature works. It deals with punishment, but not the type of symbolical mechanized punishment of "In the Penal Colony". Instead, Kafka gives us a vision of punishment growing out of a highly debatable form of justice. This vision, in the long run, was derived from the author's own guilt feelings. The **theme** of the book is the proceedings to which the main character, a bank clerk called Joseph K. (whom we shall refer to as K.) is subjected. It is important to note from the beginning that K. is no major social figure, no intellectual, no spectacular herocriminal. He is, in fact, a nondescript, unimpressive type of figure who is placed in a position which even the most brilliant, sophisticated person would find virtually impossible to manage. Kafka's choice of this character is obviously a deliberate one, since it heightens the absurdity and reinforces the tragicomedy of the whole situation.

We must not get the impression, however, that *The Trial* is in any way a philosopher's mystery story, a psychological whodunit, with K. desperately trying to discover the nature of his guilt. In a very real sense, our attention should be focused primarily on the Court of Justice, the invisible force whose presence is felt throughout the book. There are, in simplistic terms, two streams running through the book, both going in opposite directions, which try to converge but never do. One is the attempt by the Court to convince K. of his guilt, and the other is K.'s attempts to discover his own guilt. The Court does this by attempting to make inroads into K.'s conscience, make him realize his guilt, and atone for it. K., on the other hand, attempts to get right into the Court, and by so doing reach some degree of understanding as to the nature of his guilt. It is as if both are desperately pursuing each other but never meet. All this is done within the framework of what in Kafka's world is something intangible and surrealistic, yet strangely concrete and real: namely, the Law.

The fundamental paradox of the Law is made evident when we are told that K. must have been denounced, since he was arrested without having done anything wrong. But there is a law operating within the Law, formulated for K. by the Chaplain in the Cathedral who elucidates the character of this inner law when he tells K. that the Court wants nothing from him, that it allows K. to come and go as he pleases. *The Trial* can therefore be equated with the Cathedral: it is structured on law, and people come and go of their own volition. Yet there is an anomaly in this definition. If the law within the Law is something which welcomes those who come and dismisses those who want to leave, then the Court has violated its own inner injunction by having K. arrested in the first place.

Some kind of answer to the problem is found by the version of the Law given by the warder when K. was arrested. The Law, then, abuses its own inner function by arresting, and this immediately establishes in K.'s mind the idea of a fundamental contradiction between the spirit of the law within the Law and its execution. This paradox is important to recognize from the very outset, and manifests itself in the guilt-riddled attitude of the minor officials who execute the Law. They feel guilty because they know the Law is continually contradicting itself. Note Kafka's symbolic use of light throughout the novel, which he employs to reinforce this ambivalence. Twilight fills everything in the novel, which gives the dual effect of sadness and yet also of impending light. Kafka uses it in much the same way as Dickens uses fog in that other great novel concerning the law, Bleak House.

THE QUESTION OF K.'S GUILT

In the light of what we have just said, K.'s guilt is also full of paradox and ambiguity. He has apparently been arrested for negative reasons-his colorless character, his inability to love, and his banal standards-which would make him the scapegoat for modern bourgeois mediocrity. Yet the other minor officials are just as mediocre as he is, and they are not arrested. Nor can it be claimed that K.'s ignorance of the Law causes his arrest.

By all accounts K.'s life has been a model of respectability, and his trustworthiness and talents have been highly praised in his Bank. His near-hysterical confession seems to constitute what the Court might expect of him. They are, in fact, hypocritical lies, but they have not been forced out of him by the Court-which of course makes the Court innocent and K. guilty in this context.

In fact, K. has guilt feelings from the time of his arrest, but Kafka is very clever in ensuring that the reader, not K., is aware of them. The writing is of such a caliber that the reader knows that K. feels guilty at the very time he is protesting his innocence. The particularly brilliant scene between K. and Titorelli brings this out most effectively. It is almost as if someone else's overemphasis on his innocence triggers off deep-rooted guilt feelings, and that the source of K.'s feeling guilty lies in his basic unwillingness to remember what his guilt really is.

Comment

While this could lead us into a psychological study of K.'s character, we must look on the overall picture of the novel as a parable. It is noteworthy that K. comes closest to being clearly defined to K. in a Cathedral, and it is possible that Kafka deliberately chose this locale and a Christian priest for the attempt to reveal the truth to K. Yet why would Kafka, a Jew, be concerned with the mediatorship between man and God, sin and salvation, as given by Christ? To find the answer to this we should remember that Kafka was fascinated by the idea of Christ's suffering for mankind, with the awesome reminder that mankind must also suffer for Christ. For K., his suffering is without salvation, unlike Christian suffering.

K.'s guilt may well be a reflection of Kafka's own despair. It has even been suggested that K.'s inability to grasp his guilt is Kafka's way of saving that the guilt is Kafka's not K.'s. This would elucidate the incomprehensible nature of K.'s feelings. To the end, the inner, secret nature of K.'s guilt remains impenetrable and undefined, yet it permeates his nature just as the twilight seeps in everywhere in the novel.

K.'s guilt, then, must remain paradoxical, and when trying to unravel its mystery, the reader will find himself at an impasse time and time again. He will find it more rewarding, though at times equally as frustrating, to examine the paradoxical nature of the Law which arrested K., and in so doing countermanded its own inner law.

THE PARABOLIC INTERPRETATION OF THE DOORKEEPER

The doorkeeper is well worthy of study in relationship to K. and the paradox of the Law. He is an eternal figure interposed between man and the Law, and we have an immediate discrepancy here: the Law has supremacy, yet the doorkeeper seems to some the power over it. The doorkeeper is at once impressing the man with the power of the Law, yet shuns total responsibility for it by pointing out his own menial position with regard to it. He reveres the Law yet flouts it by accepting bribes. What then does Kafka mean by the doorman and the door?

Comment

Note to begin with the similarity between the doorman and the Chaplain. Both stand between man and the Law: both represent the Law yet do not fully comprehend it. Observe, too, how the doorman closes the door at the end of the parable, an action which seems to negate the statement that the Law always receives someone who wishes to enter. Also, if access to the Law and freedom to leave the Court is as easy as has been stated, why is there a door at all? Martin Buber, the Jewish theologian, has made some pungent comments on the **metaphysical** aspects of Kafka's use of the door. Buber takes a position opposite to that of most literary critics of Kafka, in that he examines K. from the vantage point of the Law, defying Kafka's own position that the Law has been lost to the world.

Kafka himself is far more interested in the doorkeeper, as is K. This is obviously because K. identifies with him and recognizes the similarities and differences of their respective positions. The priest concentrates on interpreting the doorkeeper, however, but K. can immediately identify the doorkeeper as a prototype of the emissaries of Law which have taken him into custody. The doorkeeper, like the warders and lawyers, stand as if in a doorway with their backs to the Law, representing it but unaware of its meaning. They are a part of the Court yet permanently stand apart from it.

K. AND THE TRIAL

The proceedings of the trial itself are extremely confused. The confusion is heightened by the fact that K. regards the Court as a branch of civil authority, whereas the Law seems to operate on a super human level. The fact that his contact with the Court authorities gives K. an impression of their paradoxical efficiency and bungling is not helped by the added fact that the Court operates on two levels, a hidden and an open one. Kafka adds impact to this fact by introducing some of K.'s colleagues to the scene, automatically making his secret guilt public, and making the private something universal.

Kafka makes clever use of symbolism in his setting of the trial: it is set on a July Sunday, but in the most sordid of settings. The reference to *Julius Caesar* in itself is ironical. Kafka introduces his own deep sense of class consciousness here by placing the location in a slum section, totally divorced from K.'s upper middle-class milieu.

Comment

Kafka makes subtle use of the spectators who attended the trial. Divided into three groups, they cannot be distinguished by K. as being witnesses, accused, spectators, or even jurors.

ATMOSPHERE

The atmosphere of mystery and secrecy is very cleverly set by Kafka, even to the extent of the trial's being kept secret from the Examining Magistrate and the officials themselves. The shut door, the lack of knowledge of K.'s profession, the mystery of the form of the trial are realistic elements, as opposed to symbolism, which Kafka uses to heighten the secret nature and mysterious mood of the trial itself. Symbolism is introduced again when the door is barred. K. has found himself face to face with the incomprehensible proceedings of a Law uncomprehended by officials who deny the Law's basic premise by blocking the door between an outer world and an inner world, both marked by chaos and order.

THE ROLE OF WOMEN IN THE TRIAL

If the reader studies the quality and role of women in *The Trial*, in fact, he will find that they lie within the jurisdiction of the Court, and the effect they have on K. is analogous to that of the Law itself.

Comment

Kafka's own idea of women comes into this, particularly with regard to Leni. Her role of professional helper seems to give her the air of being kind, compassionate, and affectionate. Yet she is full of inconsistencies.

Fraulein Burstner is often identified with Kafka's own fiancee, Felice Bauer. Her attitude to K. is one of frigidity and sensuality. In some strange way, too, she is implicated with the

Law, and is in many ways a personification of the Law itself. She is, like the Law, persuasively aloof yet quietly aggressive and demanding.

A third woman with whom K. comes in contact is Fraulein Montag. In their meeting, we can readily find an analogy with respect to K.'s dealings with the Law. For the elements of the Interrogation Chamber have also formed a faction of intrigue against him, and K. is left with the all-consuming impression that a major plot has united the women and the Court against him.

K'S DOWNFALL

At the point where K. abandons any attempt to reach an intellectual evaluation of justice, but starts instead to concentrate on his emotional state, Kafka turns his attention to K.'s fear of physical sickness (the autobiographical element is obvious) which temporarily gives him the idea that even his own body is being put on Trial by disease.

Even when K. is finished with the Courthouse, Kafka gives his Trial a new twist by forcing Huld and Titorelli upon him. Both the lawyer and the painter share one major quality with the Court-ambiguity.

Comment

Kafka makes subtle use of the lawyer's name here: Huld implies "unfathomable grace", and the fact that Huld transpires to be a monstrous character is Kafka's way of making a bitterly ironical commentary on any association between the Law and theological grace.

THE END

Kafka has difficulty with the end of *The Trial*, and even considered three possible conclusions. The theatricality he chose serves as a kind of **parody** of the endless flow of narrations expressing the **metaphysical** anguish and despair which torments K. to the bitter finish. Kafka's main problem was to avoid any possible interpretation that might suggest that the whole thing has been a dream.

Since the Law has from the beginning proved itself to be riddled with contradictions, K. fits into the general pattern at the conclusion. He becomes, himself, one of the puppet-like figures who have made up the structure of the Court.

Comment

Kafka makes clever symbolic use of the children K. sees before he leaves. Note that the game they play involves their not being able to touch one another, which is a rather frightening portrait of the impossibility of genuine human relationships being formed.

THE EXECUTION

A strange note is struck by the sense of elation in this instance. One cannot help thinking of the final scene in Camus' *The Stranger* at this point.

There is a sense of paradoxical symbolism about the way K. dies. The representatives of the Law apparently expect K. to perform a ritualistic, sacrificial act of self-immolation, placing the final guilt of all on his own head. Kafka brilliantly has K. put the final responsibility for his death on the shoulders of the Court.

Comment

The most puzzling aspect of the end is Kafka's reference to the "shame" that may survive K. It is difficult-virtually impossible-to find out what Kafka means by this. Several possibilities come to mind: shame at his intolerable though incomprehensible guilt; the shame of the Law's inhumanity; shame at the hidden truths of the Law which have been revealed to K.; or even shame at his own cowardice in not fulfilling the Court's tacit injunction to execute himself. Kafka leaves the question unanswered, obviously because he did not know himself. *The Trial* therefore ends on the note with which it began, and the reader is left to ponder the nature of that shame, the source of K.'s guilt, and the meaning of the monstrous and unfathomable Law that dominates Kafka's tormented world.

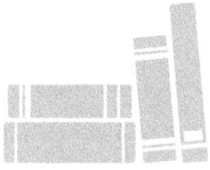

FRANZ KAFKA

THE CASTLE

GENERAL COMMENTS

Many interpretations of Kafka's novel, *The Castle*, have been offered in the past, most of them stressing the symbolism which gives the work its unique stamp. As we have pointed out before, however, a novel's literary worth cannot be too great if the reader must necessarily approach it with sound knowledge of Christian or Jewish theology or Freudian symbolism. A critic like Friedrich Beissner has approached Kafka's works from a purely literary point of view, concerning treating on such features as character delineation, language, and **imagery**. Other critics, like Max Brod, see in *The Castle* a representation of the Jewish Godhead, while others regard it as Kafka's statement on Kierkegaardian existentialist theology. To fully appreciate the work, however, the reader should not have to concentrate on any one interpretive aspect, be it theological or philosophical, but should regard it primarily as a novel. It must stand or fall basically on its intrinsic merits as a work of art, not as an intellectual treatise.

One cannot help bearing in mind, of course, certain biographical aspects of Kafka himself which had to influence his writing of the book. He was living in a kind of voluntary exile when he wrote *The Castle*, whose hero, the Land-Surveyor K., is also an expatriate. It is also interesting to note that there is an air of permanent homelessness about K., and that although he has a home, he seems to have accepted his fate as the rootless wanderer on a quest haunted by a compellingly sinister atmosphere. Much the same can be said about Kafka. Most of Kafka's **protagonists** are in some way inextricably trapped in some fashion or other: Joseph K., in *The Trial*, for example. K., however, is free to ignore whatever call or compulsion drives him to the castle.

Comment

It is true that lengthy passages in the novel are devoted to the legal aspects of K.'s position, but nevertheless he has a freedom of will which he consciously exercises.

It should also be made clear from the beginning that in dramatic terms, K. is very much the **protagonist** in this work, and that the castle itself is a most forbidding antagonist. As we have discussed, it is dangerous to see K. as a purely symbolic figure, like Bunyon's Christian or the Wandering Jew, as some commentators have interpreted him. The castle would then be seen as a clearly defined destination for the wanderer, be that destination tragic or happy.

K. cannot be fitted neatly into some preconceived theological category, and if he is, it must be as someone whose existence whirls around in an eternal demi-light somewhere between salvation and damnation. K. may be regarded as the centrifugal point of ambiguous human existence, whose paradoxical situation is not elucidated for us by Kafka. In this context the castle may well be seen as an image harboring Kafka's own profound sense of uncertainty about man's destiny - if he has one. For while K.'s wanderings suggest longing, they also imply an awesome air of futility.

KAFKA'S METHOD IN THE CASTLE

Sometimes should be said about Kafka's method of approaching whatever allegorical meaning is contained in *The Castle*. In the traditional allegory, a set of "equivalents" are usually established, by which there is a link between words and concepts. Kafka studiously avoids this method, particularly in *The Castle*, since it use would imply a concrete quality to the concept he is aiming at evoking. In a very real sense, what Kafka implies is implication itself.

Kafka as a writer leaves the reader to deal with and interpret for himself the moods which his words have provoked. The important thing to note is the atmosphere of doubt which Kafka has created - and created deliberately. The reader is left with a host of unanswered questions which he must probe for himself. If he finds answers which satisfy him, he can have no complaint.

If the reader does not satisfactory answers, he still cannot complain, for a "loose end" to one's thinking may well be what Kafka definitely meant". Kafka gives the reader a completely free choice of interpretation, and this openness of opinion is a deliberate part of the writer's method of approach.

Comment

An interesting historical note should be added here. Kafka apparently intended the novel to be written originally in the first person, and actually started writing it this way, although there is obviously a narrator who nevertheless refuses to "take sides", as it were. This narrative form in turn leads to the novel's being full of deliberately structured ambiguities.

There is consequently a state of aesthetic tension set up, whereby the objectivity of K.'s human condition is placed in juxtaposition to the subjectivity of his mental processes. This fact is a very important one for the reader to remember, since it shows Kafka's skillful use of the narrator's technique. He uses this technique with unique results, inasmuch as the reader is never in doubt as to what is going on in K.'s mind, although he is always puzzled by what is really happening and what the meaning of events really is. Kafka as narrator is thereby telling us that he has far greater insight into K. than to what happens to K. Here again he is deliberately and consciously adding to the reader's dilemma, thereby heightening the hero's plight.

AMBIGUITIES IN THE CASTLE

If one word to be used to describe the central feature of *The Castle*, that word could well be "ambiguity". This note of ambiguity is found at the very outset of the book, where the dual worlds of reality and unreality are brought starkly to the fore in the description of the castle itself. Note, too, the negative and positive attitudes achieved by Kafka in the baffling way he depicts K.'s reception at the inn. The portrait on the wall of the taproom also is used by Kafka to denote duality, tension, and ambiguity. Kafka is delivering the impact of a world in which puzzlement and awareness, reality and unreality, being and nothingness not only follow upon one another in rapid succession, but also may possibly even co-exist.

At this point it should be noted that Kafka concentrates not at all on the meaning of the castle to the reader, but entirely on what it means to the villagers and to K. Here again we run into a host of ambiguities.

Comment

K.'s remark that Klamm can be seen everywhere has often been interpreted as some kind of reference to the theological concept of immanence. This would imply that Klamm is the equivalent-in literary terms-of God. At first glance this would seem allegorically sound, since the villagers seem to talk of the castle, and of Klamm in particular, in terms that one would normally reserve for the deity. The reader must be on guard here, however, not to jump to the immediate conclusion that the castle necessarily means salvation or heaven, or that Klamm is God. For Kafka is scrupulously careful in pointing out that this is how the castle and its inhabitants appear to the villagers. In fact, the reader's suspicions are aroused when he gradually becomes aware of ambiguities in the villagers' attitudes. Not only does he not really know what goes on there, but, by subtle use of language, Kafka lets us know that hate for and fear of the castle exist in the village.

K.'S RELATIONSHIP WITH THE CASTLE

The highly personal nature of K.'s struggle is emphasized by his dim awareness that the castle may indeed contain friends as well as enemies. K.'s initial reluctance to submit himself wholly to the castle, is very important to recognize. Only then can we notice the sometimes almost imperceptible change of K.'s relationship with and attitude to the castle. Kafka also demonstrates K.'s reliance on other people's words of authority rather than his own inner convictions.

Kafka cleverly highlights K.'s increasing sense of bitterness and inferiority by forcing the reader to recognize the hero's isolation from real human contact. Kafka makes up aware of K.'s growing feelings of inferiority and guilt toward both the castle and Klamm and does so by stressing K.'s isolation and guilty posture after drinking Klamm's cognac. It seems almost as if Kafka is commenting on the guilt which man experiences when he begins to wallow in the awareness of his own inferiority and isolation.

Comment

After K.'s defeat by Klamm, we should take note of how he finds the castle's gaze almost intolerable, coupled with how he senses a stronger kind of freedom. This could be interpreted as being Kafka's way of expressing the Kierkegaardian "awareness of infinite possibility" in literary terms. For K.'s sense of being in a way liberated from conventionality and tradition immediately opens up the possibility of his someday perhaps being able to communicate with other human beings. This is linked with K.'s awareness that the castle has an objective existence in its own right, and that the difficulty of arranging a meeting with Klamm may well be associated with the fact that Klamm is superior to him. Yet Kafka carefully shows how K. can still do nothing about his situation.

K.'S CHANGE OF ATTITUDE TOWARD THE CASTLE

We should also be aware that any change of attitude on K.'s part so far does not imply a metamorphosis. It is perfectly natural that after what he has been through he should feel hostile and defiant-attitudes quite different from his near-arrogant confidence at the beginning. The interview with the official Burgel, in fact, marks the essential transformation in K.'s point of view.

K. meets Burgel feeling a desperate need for a solution. Burgel appears to assure K. that a solution is possible. Both the nature of the solution and K.'s failure to react to it lie at the core of the novel's ambiguities. Kafka achieves a literary master stroke when, at the moment when triumph-in the form of an answer-is within his grasp, K. automatically becomes oblivious to it, thereby suggesting that the solution to man's dilemma may well lie in some kind of total surrender to nature (symbolized here by sleep) marked by absence of struggle.

Burgel's explanation that an accidental meeting such as theirs holds the only chance of success may well imply that K.'s quest does definitely entail a dual process between himself and the castle. There is also the idea here that some intense struggle may be necessary before opposing powers-represented here by K. and Burgel-can attain equal strength. Why then, in view of all this, does K. not ask the essential question? Victory seems to be within his grasp, and he apparently rejects it. It is essential to note that K. is incapable of asking the question. It seems to be that had K. been able to ask the question, the answer might have been given, in which case the castle would no longer be an intriguing goal. The very fact of the answer's accessibility seems to make K. incapable of asking the question, despite the helpless position he is in.

Comment

It is interesting to note how K.'s attitude to the castle has changed. His mood of well-being, hitherto unexperienced, is translated into his joyous attitude to all around him. K.'s increasing rejection of morbid introspection and adoption of a more positive, outgoing attitude is shown by his admiration for the servant's dealings with the recalcitrant officials. What is important here is that K. has attained a certain spiritual reality marked by his recognition of the hopelessness of seeking absolute confirmation he hitherto deemed essential. Yet here again Kafka shows his brilliance by insuring that neither K. nor the reader will ever know whether the document which the servant tore up was indeed K.'s. In spite of this, the important thing to recognize is that K. no longer considers it necessary to know.

POSSIBLE INTERPRETATIONS OF K.'S CHANGE

We must be careful at this point that we do not fall back on K.'s own earlier posture of wondering whether the events which have occurred have any real significance or not. If we do this we will come to the endless skepticism of a Barnabas, who craves proof beyond all doubt, and so we must either accept K.'s transformation as being "real" or reject its reality and try to interpret what the change really means. Has some kind of victory in fact taken place?

K.'s new attitude of not reaching beneath the surface of reality to find solutions seems to suggest that he is prepared to accept varying surface realities instead. This would apparently be in line with this having abandoned attempts to reach the castle.

Kafka interjects an interesting human touch to K.'s character here by having K. try to earn the landlord's approval. He also let us know that K. is by no means a robot, sexless and devoid of feelings. Kafka also insures that we do not misinterpret K.'s apparent nonchalance as total indifference or apathy to what is around him. He makes this clear in his conversation with Pepi.

K.'s reply to Pepi has been compared to something stated by Kierkegaard in his Concluding Unscientific Postscript: "Within the individual man there is a potentiality... which is awakened in inwardness to become a God-relationship, and then it becomes possible to see God everywhere". The change in K.'s attitude in fact reflects a fundamental metamorphosis in his disposition. He now thinks that good will exists in the castle and all around him. We should note that this change has been neither earned by his merits, nor has it been won in struggle against the castle. One of the more plausible interpretations of the meaning of K.'s transformation has been given by Ronald Gray in his Kafka's Castle. He suggests that it represents man's entry into a state of grace, while making the strict reservations that the castle per se in all its details does not compare identically with the "seat of grace".

Comment

It is suggested that in *The Castle* K. struggles to find some definitive, objective confirmation of his own private judgment. After a quest which leads him to frustration, hatred, and morbid introspection, he seems suddenly to become a sympathetic, understanding figure. This change has taken place somehow because of K.'s relationship with the castle, although the castle is not in itself a final authority. K. is forced into a position of spiritual immobility, a condition which demands that he wait things out, albeit against his will. When he gave up the struggle completely, his reality was changed as by a miracle. Yet this is not to be regarded as an "act of grace" in any Christian sense, since

K.'s certainty is achieved through unawareness, and has not removed the possibility that doubt or skepticism may well still exist in him. There are, of course, many other interpretations, some of which we will discuss shortly.

THE NOVEL FROM VIEWPOINTS OTHER THAN K.'S

Up to this point we have been discussing aspects of *The Castle* as seen through the eyes of K. Yet the whole picture is not complete, and the apparently unconnected series of events have no harmony, unless we can examine the story from angles other than K.'s. Take, for example, the events following K.'s abandonment by his assistants. From K.'s point of view, he cannot possibly comprehend any kind of meaning or any degree of unity in the anomalous events. But we have seen that, from the reader's point of view, this may well be interpreted as K.'s being made aware of his own insignificance, having his humility tested, and receiving a measure of reward. This is certainly but one interpretation which cannot be made by K., who has to wait and accept what happens.

K. is, in a very real sense, the victim of his disposition, but he cannot see that the villagers are also. We must not forget, in fact, that much of the hostility, whether real or not, which K. feels is directed toward him has nothing to do with the castle itself. From another angle, K. finds it exceedingly difficult to accept that he might be wrong about people's attitudes, and when experiences do prove him wrong, he accepts this almost against his will. His first impression of the schoolmaster, for example, is that he is a domineering, pompous type of man, and K. is surprised to hear him talking in a mild tone of voice. Note, too, how unwilling K. is to accept the fact that he has indeed many friends at the castle, and it is not until he has undergone the whole terrifying experience of feeling totally isolated that Kafka tells us K. has become more mild.

Comment

In order to achieve an overall picture of what is actually happening, the reader must take into consideration K.'s mood, together with the tone of the reaction he encounters. When we are told, for example, that the villagers seem hostile or friendly, this is admittedly a statement of how K. feels. But it also suggests the distinct possibility that the villagers may be hostile or friendly indeed, as the case may be. We must not forget also that Kafka sometimes inserts scenes which are deliberately shrouded in mystery, and which defy a completely satisfactory explanation irrespective of what vantage point we take.

Kafka, of course, writes in such a way that the reader first and foremost receives the impact of events as seen through the eyes of the main character. The reader, however, must then work to interpret the causal links and interpretive chains which join together ostensibly unrelated events. This is sometimes imaginatively and intellectually demanding, since these links lie often in **metaphysical** realms which are extremely difficult to define.

FRIEDA, GARDENA, AND K.

The implications surrounding K.'s encounters with Frieda and Gardena are worthy of studying for the light they throw on the idea of progress in *The Castle*. These two subsidiary characters are in a different relationship to the castle than is K. K.'s relationship to these two characters should be studied closely by the reader, who might find similarities between these meetings and K.'s interview with Burgel, inasmuch as K.'s position to them is close to what Burgel is to K. Both sets of relationships imply an involvement in which each party furthers or promotes the other.

Comment

From Kafka's point of view as a novelist, K.'s encounters with Frieda and Gardena at once serve to highlight the aspects of the quest we have just discussed, and make more frighteningly significant the general retreat of the world from K. For it is now that the reader appreciates the involuted nature of K.'s quest, made more terrible by his increasing isolation, and more apparently futile by the "mass retreat" of external reality before K.'s very eyes.

OLGA, AMALIA AND K.

Olga and Amalia are two interesting characters, inasmuch as they represent the results of refusal to obey the castle, which is represented to K. in the worst possible light when Barnabas' family history is recounted. Many diverse theological interpretations have been made by Olga's version of this history.

At this point we shall not go into all the details of the various interpretations of this history which have been given, although a brief glance at some of them will show the reader how Kafka's simplest passages can contain remarkable profundities. Max Brod, for example, compares the Sortini episode with the **theme** of Kierkegaard's *Fear and Trembling*, which presents the argument that God asked Abraham to commit a crime, namely the sacrifice of his child. Brod sees Sortini's command to Amalia as God's command to Abraham, both representing the gross injustices of divine authority when judged by human standards.

Ronald Gray criticizes Brod for misinterpreting Kierkegaard, claiming that the philosopher's point of view and Kafka's are indeed similar, but only to the extent of Abraham's and K.'s "unawareness".

Erich Heller, on the other hand, attacks Brod for blasphemy, accusing him of insulting the intelligence of the reader. We shall examine this issue in detail later, but it should be pointed out now as a word of warning that to find any kind of definitive solution to this problem would pretty much demand a complete examination of the problem of good and evil.

The characters of Amalia and Olga are worthy of study to give us some clue as to what Kafka meant by their presence in the novel. Amalia apparently has all the trappings of virtue, inasmuch as she is patient, sincere, long-suffering, and makes decisions for her family. Yet her presence, with its solemn, almost noble features, is oppressive to K., which is perhaps linked in some way with the fact that Amalia's form of stoicism leads her to embrace her terrible isolation proudly and with dignity. In this way she does in fact resemble the Abraham discussed by Kierkegaard, in that her refusal to accept Sortini and the serenity with which she accepts her isolation can be equated with Abraham's acceptance of God's inhuman ways.

Olga, on the other hand, is unlike Amalia in several respects: she does not share Amalia's rigidity of attitude: she has had no evidence of the good will of the castle, and has been met by the hostility of the villagers and indifference of the castle in the face of the many appeals she has made. Yet she has great faith in the castle and believes that its actions can be equated with an attitude of love.

Comment

It is not a question for K. of having to decide on the moral rightness or wrongness of both positions. He prefers Olga for the virtues of her disposition, yet can still find reasons for defending Amalia. Note that Kafka very carefully refuses in any way to help the reader take sides in the question of moral rightness. What he makes clear, however, are the consequences of accepting or refusing Sortini's command, the dual attitudes shown in Olga's and Amalia's responses, and the effect these responses have on K. It is important to note that the attitude preferred by K. is that of Olga, whose serene peace of mind and faith in the castle depends not on shallowness of insight, but on a firm belief in the existence and efficacy of love.

THE COUNT AND K.

Any attempt to find a solution to the real meaning of the castle must necessarily involve some discussion of its "real" master, described in the first chapter as "Count Westwest". This in turn must lead to an examination of the nature of the castle's inner chamber. Erich Heller has gone so far as ascribing to the castle officials the qualities of Gnostic demons, while Georg Lukacs claims that the real administration of the castle represents "the transcendence of Kafka's allegories", namely nothingness. This would seem to justify K.'s first impression of the castle's emptiness, and would further justify the claim that the only thing certain about the castle's central authority is its absolute negation. If this interpretation is valid, the Count is an un-god, the non-materialistic personification of atheism.

An examination of the name given by Kafka to the Count has revealed some interesting observations, the most valid of which seems to be that the writer was being deliberately mysterious. The critic Emrich has suggested that the word "west" suggests the sunset world beyond death, the absolute end, and yet that it also may well represent the conquest of death. It is interesting to note, however, that the word "west" is repeated in the Count's name, which could imply the end of the decline, which would infer some kind of ascendancy. If this is the case, the ruler of the castle would represent to Kafka some image of eternal life or resurrection - the kind of idea expressed in Dylan Thomas' "Death Shall Have No Dominion". None of these explanations is totally satisfactory, however, since there is always some aspect of the novel which arises to negate what has been established.

Perhaps the most credible answer is one that would embrace a duality of interpretations, in which case Count Westwest would represent both negation and resurrection, life and death, heaven and hell-something akin to what Eugene O'Neill called "hopeless hope". This in many ways would provide some degree of satisfactory answer to the puzzling, anomalous, and ambiguous aspects of *The Castle*. When K. wavers between fear and hope, uncertainty and arrogance, doubt and certitude, it would appear that the object of his quest - ultimately Count Westwest-may epitomize all these dualities. K.'s subjective ambivalence could be explained by his having the state of mind that craves something desperately, but feels threatened by the fear that if his wishes are fulfilled, some kind of termination will ensue which he does not want.

Kafka's use of images regarding the Count's identity are worth studying. The bells of the castle, for example, are described as if they were church bells, pealing merrily and filling K. with the tremblings of a strange, vaguely defined desire. This is immediately followed, however, by a weak, tedious little tinkling sound, which not only is the antithesis of the first image, but which also is not definitely from the castle. When Kafka says that the sound might have come from anywhere in the village, he is giving a deliberately blurred effect to what the bells represent.

Comment

This duality of motif, ambiguity of **theme**, and perplexity of content is in some ways the hallmark of *The Castle*. Yet far from being a deterrent to its success, the paradoxes the novel contains make it one of the most intriguing novels ever written. If the reader finds a satisfactory answer to its riddles, or if he remains baffled, the book still stands as a masterpiece. For in the long run, it stands on its own merits as a literary work of art, not as a **metaphysical** treatise.

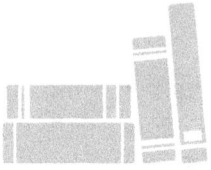

FRANZ KAFKA

AMERIKA

GENERAL COMMENTS

Published posthumously under the title *Amerika*, this novel was originally entitled *The Boy Who Was Never More Heard Of*. To understand its full importance, the reader should be aware of Kafka's own interest in socialism and its place in a capitalist society. As a young student, he interested himself in movements dealing with social and political freedom, although he never actually joined any party. His nature was such that he could not adhere totally to any socialist group because of his natural tendency toward outspoken criticism - for example, seen in their widest context, his works are violent protests against the unseen forces of the universe which paralyze man's spirit. From a human point of view, however, Kafka deplored the miseries he saw around him as a result of social abuses. Yet *Amerika* is by no means to be regarded as a novel of "social realism", for the reality it contains has overtones which go beyond the literature of social protest.

The opening of the novel alone, which introduces us to the hero, Karl Rossmann, gives a dual atmosphere of speed and immobility, symbolizing the permanent reality and fleeting illusions of the New World. Note how the Statue of Liberty is seen as some kind of mythical goddess, and how her torch is seen as a sword - the immediate implication being that Karl's sense of liberty is somehow confused with violence and perhaps even revenge. It should be made clear, however, that the opening chapter, "The Stoker", is not intended in any way as an attack on the social injustices Karl will encounter in America. The sword is pointed at Rossmann's conscience rather than at America's ills.

Kafka can be faulted at this point, however, for the too-rapid transition he makes from reality to the sub-strata of reality -an art which, with maturity, he developed to a masterful precision. His description of Uncle Jacob's business, for example, is a brilliantly concise indictment of the dehumanizing process of the modern business world. Yet it seems somehow divorced from the central figure, Karl, whom Kafka imbues with a sense of nostalgic social compassion that seems to emanate from Kafka himself, rather than from his sixteen-year-old hero. It is almost as if Kafka injects into Karl emotions which Kafka himself thinks he might have felt as an emigrant of Karl's age. Despite these anomalies, however, it should be kept in mind that *Amerika* is primarily not about America, but about the growth of Karl Rossmann.

KARL AND THE STOKER

Many misinterpretations have been applied to the word "infantilism" with regard to Karl's character. Only if we regard the word as meaning immaturity in his case will we be able to reach some comprehension of his attitudes. We must beware of viewing Karl as the guileless innocent whose goodness is ineffectual set against the corruption of American capitalistic society. To do so would be to miss the whole point of the paradoxes inherent in the story and the dark guilts that are continually straining in Karl's character for clarification. Karl's problem is to find stability in a fluctuating world and to sort out the nature of guilt and innocence in an environment ruled by primitive morality. The sword now takes on the symbolic significance of a sword of justice, with Karl both guilty and innocent, unable to extricate himself from the coils of an incomprehensible retribution.

Kafka's use of symbolism is noteworthy. Karl has descended from the sunlight to the darkness, where he encounters the huge Stoker. The Stoker is reminiscent of Joanna in his brutish sexuality, his sullenness, and his menial position; both have religious symbols on their walls.

Two trials take place. The one is almost over before it begins. The other, much more subtle, concerns the whole principle of justice, which is itself on trial.

From a character point of view, Kafka throws some cruelly stark light on the subconscious motivations that prompt Karl's actions. His pathetic failure in the trial underscores a basic point that Kafka seems to be making, which is that Karl's banishment was somehow justified.

Comment

Kafka uses symbolism in having Karl descend the rope ladder to America, just as he descended to meet the Stoker. We will see also how he descends from high society to the company of vagabonds. This use of the Fall was a very conscious one on Kafka's part. Karl's sobs as he leaves with his uncle reinforce

Kafka's contention that man's tragedy lies, in his preference for the evil into which he can descend so readily. This is the curse of man's freedom, which adds further meaning to the sword in the hand of the Statue of Liberty.

KARL AND THE HOTEL OCCIDENTAL

Kafka deliberately confuses us as to the amount of time spent between Karl's odyssey from the boat, his expulsion from his uncle's house, to the Hotel Occidental where he himself stands trial. The author very cleverly gives the impression, however, that in a symbolic sense Karl has not progressed far and that he still lives in the shadow of the sword. A dreamlike atmosphere of rebirth is created for the boy, but everything he sees seems to evoke memories of the Old World to the extent of his being frustrated in his attempts to relish the miracles he sees before him.

Comment

The daydream in which Karl indulges may not be quite so innocuous as it seems. His fantasy may be an attempt to dethrone a preconceived father image. The delivery of the traveling box symbolizes, quite literally, that Karl cannot escape the decay of the Old World and all its familial connotations.

There is even symbolism in the name of Karl's next abode and with an atmosphere of historical decline and decay.

Worth studying is the powerful and deeply moving account of the death of Therese's mother, which happens to be one of the finest prose passages Kafka ever wrote. In it he combines

realism and surrealism, beauty and tragedy, with a deep-rooted sense of social injustice as seen through the eyes of a young girl.

Karl's being given the apple on the evening of his fall has the painfully obvious symbolism of his being a new Adam. It receives a subtle twist in the hands of Kafka, who carefully avoids having Karl either eat the fruit or fall in love. Karl's fall has already been assured, and Therese's gesture is but a bitterly futile one.

KARL AND HIS TRIAL

Kafka's depiction of Karl looking down into the light shaft suggests his impending plunge into deeper guilt and punishment. On one level Karl genuinely wishes to come to terms with authority, yet on another he is continually rebelling against it. His words therefore contradict his thoughts as he tries to explain himself to the Head Waiter. He resents the authority opposing him on the grounds that there is no good will involved. Authority to Karl apparently must show understanding before it has any claim to chastising.

Karl's conceptions of abstract justice are again shattered when the Manageress informs him that if one can arrange things to look right, expediency will supersede justice. Karl's experience with the trial of the Stoker makes him opt to placate his adversary, thus immediately contradicting his own lofty ideals of justice. Note how brilliantly Kafka equates Karl's trial with the Stoker's: both are trapped by their backgrounds; both are essentially asocial figures; both are ineffectually defended; both cave in and admit their guilt. This paradox of sophistication and naivete is typical of the Kafka hero.

Comment

The powerful scene when Karl is about to leave is closely akin to the symbolism surrounding the door in *The Trial*. There is always some authority symbol, some insignificant underling, who represents and enforces the Law without comprehending it. His quest for justice, freedom, truth, and everything meant by the myth of the New World has ended in negation, a spiritual vacuum, a bleak world where disillusionment and nihilism reign supreme.

THE END

The locale of the final scene has great symbolic significance, although its nature remains a mystery until the very end. Some critics see it as some kind of **metaphysical** Mecca to which Karl has made his final pilgrimage, while two others it represents salvation in the form of the Catholic Church. It has been argued that it is the theatre of truth, where revelations of ultimate answers are enacted for Karl's benefit. The only thing certain is that the theatre has allegorical significance, although Kafka was working on so many levels at this point that any definitive interpretation is virtually impossible. The cheap religious trappings and the actors combine to give the atmosphere of ethereal theatricality. Kafka is obviously attempting to create a theatre of illusion set in a world of grim reality.

Comment

The theatre, then, represents the apex of Karl's American experience, a world of illusion and disillusionment, but nevertheless one which he desperately wishes to enter. In the employment bureau, it is improbable that Kafka was indulging in any kind of social criticism concerning the Negro problem in America. The word "Negro" had been given to Karl, undoubtedly as an indication of his feelings of total alienation and degradation, and the fact that he uses it now is an indication of his desperate need for acceptance.

Instead of being a place of welcome, the theatre is transformed into a kind of Court, where Karl is being continually tested. He is again made to feel his sense of being an alien who will never be fully accepted. The Head, who reveals the deception and illusion under which Karl operates, seems to represent his past. The clerk, on the other hand, may well represent Karl's future-and note how he "graduates",: in a sense, under false pretenses and as the result of an act of insubordination on the part of the clerk. But even Karl's "commencement" is a down-grading experience, for his progress really transpires to be retrogression.

It is also important to note that at the very end he is not even accepted by his name but merely as an anonymous non-being about to be transported to some nameless, amorphous destination. He has indeed become "The Boy Who Was Never More Heard Of". Both Joseph K. and Karl Rossmann find a destination which, in its terrifying anonymity, seems the only one possible for those tormented by guilt and haunted by innocence.

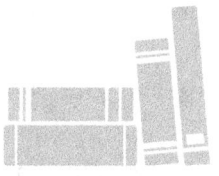

FRANZ KAFKA

COMMENTARY

KAFKA AND LITERARY CRITICISM

Kafka is indeed an extremely difficult writer to comprehend, and the surface enjoyment of his works can and indeed must be penetrated if the reader wishes to enrich his own aesthetic experience. In this case, it is advisable to turn to the professional critics who have attempted to analyze his works. On the whole, these critics have approached Kafka the novelist, by examining such aspects of his work as **imagery**, character delineation, language and so forth. This approach does not negate the fact of Kafka's being a profoundly religious writer, however, for he is. What it does do is illuminate the religiously allegorical aspects of his works by inspecting the novels and stories of Kafka first, rather than delving straight into their spiritual or **metaphysical** content. Let it be stressed that we are not in any way negating or minimizing the sterling work accomplished by critics whose view of Kafka is one confined to religion. What is being suggested, nevertheless, is the fact that such a specialized interpretation limits our vision of Kafka as a literary artist, giving us a picture of him as a kind of Freudian mystic who happened to be a writer.

W. H. Auden deplores the fact that Kafka belongs to the "cultist" school, and in discussing the philosophical problems inherent in Kafka's works, deals at length with the problem of the Quest. Auden stresses the fact that the real significance of any neurosis is teleological in nature, and that the problems with which Kafka grappled have in fact nothing to do with his father. According to Auden, Kafka's own quest took the form of a tormented struggle between his skepticism and his burning personal need for faith.

Max Brod says, "In the case of Franz Kafka, this fate cannot be considered so cruel, since he was a man utterly indifferent to fame. Writing was for him a 'form of prayer' (as he put it in one of his diaries). His efforts were directed toward inner perfection, toward a stainless life. It was not that he did not care what the world thought of him; rather, he simply had not time to worry about it. For he was wholly occupied with the striving for the highest ethical pinnacle a man can attain - a pinnacle which in truth scarcely can be attained. He was filled with a drive, intensified to the point of pain and semi-madness, not to brook any vice in himself, any lie, any self-deception, nor any offense against his fellow men - this passion for perfection often took the form of self-humiliation, since Kafka saw his own weaknesses as though under a microscope, magnified to many times their size. How he despaired of himself on account of these weaknesses, longing as he did for intimate fusion with the Pure, the Divine, which in his aphorisms he described as the 'Indestructible.' This ideal preoccupied him throughout his life. In this sense Kafka, of all modern writers, is the one most closely akin to Tolstoi. "Man cannot live without a lasting trust in something indestructible within himself - in this sentence Kafka formulated his religious position".

Martin Buber, having examined the parable "Before the Law", expands his ideas into some general comments about *The Trial*, saying that the novel describes "a district delivered over to the authority of a slovenly bureaucracy without the possibility of appeal . . . What is at the top of the government, or rather above it, remains hidden in a darkness, of the nature of which one never once gets a presentment; the administrative hierarchy, who exercise power, received it from above, but apparently without any commission or instruction . . . Man is called into this world, he is appointed in it, but wherever he turns to fulfill his calling he comes up against the thick vapors of a mist of absurdity . . . - it is a Pauline world, except that God is removed into the impenetrable darkness and that there is no place for a mediator".

Edwin Berry Burgum takes a uniquely Marxist standpoint in his appraisal of Kafka's works, making such assertions as the following: ". . . his attempt to escape a dominating father left his adolescence stranded upon the fluctuating shoals of the Weimar Republic"; "His own diseased personality structure symbolized the disease at the heart of German society"; "He takes us into the personality structure itself, remaining unconscious of its nature since he shares it"; "Kafka's last stories are almost exclusively devoted to his hallucinations"; "That Kafka's anxieties have passed the norm and become psychotic in 'The Burrow' is obvious"; and "K.'s murder symbolizes the final ascendancy of fascism. . . ".

Bergum also regards Kafka as being essentially a religious man, perhaps even a mystic. Yet he does not necessarily mean to praise Kafka by describing him this way. He says of him that "like Kierkegaard, his favorite philosopher, he represents the breakdown of mysticism itself, both as a discipline and as a philosophy. In the light of the great religious mystics of history, to emphasize Kafka's religious mysticism can only mean to share his own incapacity for reasoned judgment".

Albert Camus says: "It would indeed be intelligent to consider as inevitable the progression leading from *The Trial* to *The Castle*. Joseph K. and the Land Surveyor K. are merely two poles that attract Kafka. I shall speak like him and say that his work is probably not absurd. But that should not deter us from seeing its nobility and universality. They come from the fact that he managed to represent so fully the everyday passage from hope to grief and from desperate wisdom to intentional blindness. His work is universal (a really absurd work is not universal) to the extent to which it represents the emotionally moving face of man fleeing humanity, deriving from his contradictions reasons for believing, reasons for hoping from his fecund despairs, and calling life his terrifying apprenticeship in death. It is universal because its inspiration is religious. As in all religions, man is freed of the weight of his own life. But if I know that, if I can even admire it, I also know that I am not seeking what is universal, but what is true. The two may well not coincide".

Pavel Eisner says that "Kafka's books are tragedies of loneliness, of hermetic isolation, of the curse of existence which converts the concrete individual into an enigmatic outcast. A person desires recognition in society, before the 'law,' in the workaday relations of civil life; but he is foreign and remains so, merely tolerated, pushed aside, reinstated, but never on the way to complete assimilation; always on the edge, a marginal settler, burdened with an invisible leprosy; but at the same time almost sacer, in the ancient paradoxical sense of the word, which encompasses a range of meaning from 'elect' and 'holy' to 'cursed' and 'damned.' That is *The Castle* of Kafka. Or a person is tried by an invisible tribunal. It drives him to justify himself, although no one constrains him to do so. For a long time the proceedings are suspended; but finally they end with a declaration of 'Guilty!' and an infamous execution. That is *The Trial* of Kafka.

Ezequiel Estrada regards Kafka's works as explorations in the mysticism of intuition, making the following observations: "The most direct route to an interpretation of Kafka is not that which leads straight to conclusions . . ". Calling intuition the "new technique for understanding and divining the nature of the world,: he says that Kafka "applies the new tool of pure intuition to the observation and chronicling of the reality of man in an alien world". Estrada places Kafka's works in a revolutionary category, inasmuch as Kafka's use of intuition divided the new world of relativity and the universe of neovitalism.

Ronald Gray attacks critics who approach Kafka as if he were a priest or a psychologist. He says: "This attitude ignores the possibility that Kafka worked as a literary artist, not inventing complex equivalents for a system of beliefs already held, but exploring the possibilities of an image which presented itself to his imagination, in this case the image of a castle and of a man trying to reach it. The ramified account of such an image has to remain consistent with itself, but not, as a primary requirement, with such conceptions as other people's ideas on the nature of God, or on the influence of childhood experience on religious belief".

Erich Heller claims that there is a certain amount of what he calls "religious relevance" about *The Castle*, but says, "It is hard to see how *The Castle* can possibly be called a religious allegory with a pilgrim of the type of Bunyan's as its hero". His claim is that since neither K. nor Kafka make any progress, there can be no comparison with Bunyan's hero. He goes on to say, "The castle of Kafka's novel is, as it were, the heavily fortified garrison of a company of Gnostic demons, successfully holding an advanced position against the maneuvers of an impatient soul. I do not know of any conceivable idea of divinity which could justify those interpreters who see in the castle the residence of 'divine law and divine grace.'" Heller admits, then, that *The Castle* may be about a religious quest, but it would be wrong to regard it in any way as a religious allegory.

Kalus Mann says, "Kafka, for all his aristocratic reserves, was not spared awkward misinterpretations. He has been identified with the Surrealists, and with a certain decadent Viennese school, there were even attempts at analyzing from a Marxist angle certain enigmatic passages in his books. All such interpretations are, of course, erroneous, and utterly fail to define the true substance of his being and writing. He never meant to surprise and startle his readers by macabre tricks. He wanted to be plastic, plain and simple. His literary masters were Flaubert and Tolstoi rather than Baudelaire and Dostoievski. He has been compared with Edgar Allan Poe, but he admired Dickens. His supreme ambition was to describe the dismay and ecstasy of his inward adventures as thoroughly and realistically as Flaubert described all the details of Madame Bovary's appearance, or Tolstoi the face and smell of a Russian peasant. Kafka is no surrealist but the most realistic explorer of spheres that are not less real for their being inaccessible to average travelers".

Thomas Mann, in a homage to Kafka, says, "But though his gaze makes us conceive of him as a Novalis from the east of Europe, yet I should not care to dub Kafka either a romantic, an ecstatic, or a mystic. For a romantic he is too clear-cut, too realistic, too well attached to life and to a simple, native effectiveness in living. His sense of humor-of an involved kind peculiar to himself-is too pronounced for an ecstatic. And as for mysticism: he did indeed once say, in a conversation with Rudolf Steiner, that his own work had given him understanding of certain 'clairvoyant states' described by the latter. And he compared his own work with 'a new secret doctrine, a cabala.' But there is lacking to it the hot and heavy atmosphere of transcendentalism; the sensual does not pass over into the super-sensual, there is no 'voluptuous hell,' no 'bridal bed of the tomb,' nor the rest of the stock-in-trade of the genuine mystic. None of that was in his line; neither Wagner's Tristan nor Novalis's "Hymns to the Night" nor his love for his dead Sophie would have appealed to Kafka. He was a dreamer, and his compositions are often dreamlike in conception and form; they are as oppressive, illogical, and absurd as dreams, those strange shadow-pictures of actual life. But they are full of reasoned morality, an ironic, satiric, desperately reasoned morality, struggling with all its might toward justice, goodness, and the will of God. All that mirrors itself in his style: a conscientious, curiously explicit, objective, clear, and correct style, which in its precise, almost official conservatism is reminiscent of Adalbert Stifter's. Yes, he was a dreamer; but in his dreaming he did not yearn after a 'blue flower' blossoming somewhere in a mystical sphere; he yearned after the 'blisses of the commonplace.'"

Edwin Muir regarded the works of Kafka as being definitely metaphysical or theological in nature. He went so far as to place them in the same category as the *Pilgrim's Progress*, with the distinction that Kafka's religious allegories were more complex, ambiguous, and highly personal. Muir, unlike Max Brod, was unhappy with any kind of pragmatic interpretation of the word 'divine' when used in relation to Kafka's works. He went to great pains to try to prove that Kafka's works fall into the category of mystical revelations.

Charles Neider claims that Kafka is a conscious satirist. He says, "Kafka's works are attacks on cabalas", meaning "the mystical school-by far the greatest cabala of them all". He says that Kafka's works constitute a **satire** on irrationalism; for example, he claims that "a satire on cabalism permeates *The Castle*", and that "Kafka's fable in *The Trial* as well as in the rest of his work is the education of all youthful idealists into adjusted middle-aged 'realists.'"

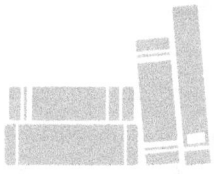

FRANZ KAFKA

ESSAY QUESTIONS AND ANSWERS

Question: Discuss some of the relationships between Kafka's *The Trial* and Camus' *The Stranger*.

Answer: To begin with, both novels are related in unique ways to the idea of crime and punishment, the fundamental difference being that K. is punished for a crime which is undefined while Meursault committed the crime of murder. Camus wrote his novel in such a way, however, that Meursault's crime was the result of other hidden forces which, paradoxically, imply that he is in a sense both guilty and innocent. In this sense we can see an immediate link between Kafka's novel and Camus': the ambiguity of innocence and guilt as well as the incongruous aspects of crime and punishment. Both heroes have also displayed an indifference toward their mothers, which, while it does not imply a source of guilt, at least suggests that the two men have in some way cut themselves off from their origins. In both cases this affects their attitudes to women.

There are, of course, differences between the two men, and if we examine the way in which each deals with the priest sent to them by the authorities that have condemned them, some of these differences are brought into sharp relief. Meursault is adamant in his refusal to see the priest, while K. seems to have been lured in some way into the Cathedral where he encounters the Chaplain. While neither man is willing to seek solace in religion, their attitudes are different. Meursault is outspoken and K. is reticent. Meursault sees his crime as an offense against society for which he has to pay the supreme price, and cannot accept the priest's claim that the law which has condemned him is but a tangible manifestation of some supreme, divine Authority. Yet the essence of both men's guilt is in some way distorted by the Law, which is incomprehensible in its inner meaning, yet thoroughly effective when it comes to meting out punishment, warranted or unwarranted. To Joseph K., this perversion is another manifestation of the chaos and corruption of a society already doomed by a vast, cruel **metaphysical** disorder which blights humanity.

There was, of course, a fundamental difference in the positions adopted by Camus and Kafka themselves. Camus was convinced, at the time he wrote *The Stranger*, that we inhabit a godless world which can nonetheless prevail through the unique dignity of the human spirit. This explains why Kafka's hero is riddled with unanswerable questions, paradoxes, and ambiguities, while Meursault is insistent on the fact of his "rightness". It has been argued that Meursault's protests are but those of a trapped and doomed man, but they are in fact the subjective protests against an objective foe, the Law, which apparently operates on a basis of psychologically subjective motivations. In both trials, for example, there is an undisputed atmosphere of sadism in the Law which confronts the two men. The law as mirrored by the two clergymen is one based on a pre-Nietzschean theology which has clear-cut answers finding expression in Law. But this is incomprehensible and untenable to post-Nietzschean figures who find themselves alienated and rootless in a world which by its very structure is destined to victimize them. In this sense, then, both Joseph K. and Meursault are indeed innocent victims.

The two works were particularly fascinating for the disillusioned generation which found itself after the Second World War in an atmosphere akin to that experienced by both Meursault and K. This situation arose not because of any answers given in the books - for there are none - but rather for the terrifying questions raised by them. When K. defies the Court, his scorn is meaningless and even has the hint of his acceptance of the Court's judgment. Note one fundamental difference here between K. and Meursault, however. At the end, Meursault remembers his mother, and remembers her with the emotion of sympathy. In this alone, Camus affirmed his faith in the human spirit, a faith that is absent in the bleak wilderness of Kafka's world.

Question: Discuss the importance and implications of the Sortini **episode** in *The Castle*.

Answer: Max Brod, Kafka's friend and biographer, draws a parallel between this **episode** and the central **theme** of Kierkegaard's *Fear and Trembling*, in which he equates Sortini's command to Amalia with God's order to Abraham. The critic Erich Heller violently disagrees with this interpretation, going so far as to accuse Brod of blasphemy. Heller goes on to claim that the castle stands as an obstruction to K.'s progress, rather than his ultimate goal. Yet can one take either position and come to a clear-cut conclusion, in view of the ambiguities that exist not only in Kafka's novel, but also in the Biblical account of Abraham and Isaac? It is probable that God was not trying to prove Abraham's guilt, but that he was putting his faith to a test. Kafka obviously did not insert the incident with Amalia with no symbolic significance in mind. It has often been suggested, in fact, that the nature of Sortini's command suggests a grossness and an intrinsic immorality which, since he is an official, may well characterize the true nature of the castle itself.

Now, to get back to Brod's interpretation and Heller's refutation of it, one cannot help observing that God's injunction to Abraham, according to Kierkegaard, falls into the same category as Sortini's command to Amalia. It was, by human standards, an unfair and even cruel order to sacrifice Abraham's most precious possession. In this respect, there is a parallel between the Sortini **episode** and Kierkegaard's interpretation of the Abraham story. It is essentially a story of conflict between one's sense of personal dignity and one's sense of duty to obey an injunction from a divine authority, harsh and meaningless as that injunction may appear. There is a further similarity between Amalia's position and that of Abraham as viewed by Kierkegaard. By refusing to obey the command and thereby retaining their sense of integrity and honor, they are automatically placed in a position of existential isolation. In this respect Kafka expressed in dramatic and poignant terms the terrible outcome of a dilemma which has been resolved in one sense but which in another sense will always remain unsolved. For Amalia-and the reader-will never know what would have happened had she accepted. Acceptance could have led to her damnation, it is true; but it might also have led to her eternal salvation.

SUGGESTED ESSAY TOPICS

1. To what extent does Kafka succeed in concealing any social, political, and religious criticisms which his works may contain?

2. Discuss the historical framework within which Kafka's three novels were written, paying particular attention to

the literary **genres** prevalent in contemporary European literature and the effects which Kafka's works had on postwar trends.

3. In what respects are K. in *The Castle* and Joseph K. in *The Trial* similar and different?

4. Discuss the religious symbolism contained in Kafka's novels, paying particular attention to the diverse views of Jewish and Christian theologians who have attempted interpretations of Kafka's works.

5. If one were to take a totally classical Freudian interpretation of Kafka's major works, what details in the lives of K., Joseph K., and Karl Rossmann would you select for study and examination?

6. Write a first-person account of the Penal Colony as seen through the eyes of (a) the Explorer, (b) a prisoner condemned to die, and (c) the new Commandant.

7. Attempt to reconstruct, in essay form, Gregor Samsa's life up to the evening before his metamorphosis.

8. Assuming that Count Westwest is a person, write an imaginary account of all his meetings, orders, and the information he receives, in relation to K.'s arrival in the village.

9. Discuss Kafka's symbolic use of names in his writings.

10. Can *Amerika*, *The Trial*, and *The Castle* justifiably be described as a trilogy? If so, what are the comprehensive links that unify them?

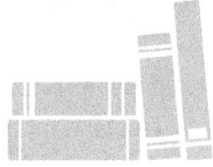

THE TRIAL AND OTHER WORKS

BIBLIOGRAPHY

Kafka's Life

Brod, Max, *Franz Kafka, A Biography,* Eng. tr., 1947.

The Diaries of Franz Kafka (ed. by Max Brod), 2 Vol., Eng. tr., 1948-9.

General Criticism And Interpretation

Carrouges, M., *Franz Kafka,* 1948.

Flores, Angel, *Franz Kafka Today,* ed. Angel Flores and Homer Swander, 1958.

Goodman, Paul, *Kafka's Prayer,* 1947.

Hubben, W., *Four Prophets of Our Destiny,* 1952.

The Kafka Problem, ed. by Angel Flores, 1946.

Neider, Charles, *The Frozen Sea: A Study of Franz Kafka,* 1948.

Politzer, Heinz, *Franz Kafka: Parable and Paradox,* 1962.

Scott, N.A., *Rehearsals of Discomposure,* 1952.

The German Novel

Bithell, Jethro, *Modern German Literature,* 1880-1950, 1959.

Heller, Erich, *The Disinherited Mind,* 1952.

Lange, Victor, *Modern German Literature,* 1870-1940, 1945.

Morgan, Bayard Quincy, *A Critical Bibliography of German Literature in English translation,* 1938.

Pascal, Roy, *The German Novel,* 1956.

Robertson, J.G., *A History of German Literature,* 1959.

Samuel, Richard and R. Hinton Thomas, *Expressionism in German Life, Literature and the Theatre,* 1910-1924, 1939.

Articles

Arendt, H., "Franz Kafka", Partisan Review, XI, 1944, pp. 412-422.

Belgion, M., "Kafka", Criterion, XVIII, 1938, pp. 13-28.

Brod, M., "Franz Kafka's Letter to His Father", Transition, no. 27, 1938, pp. 295-313.

Kelly, J., "Franz Kafka's Trial and the Theology of Crisis", *Southern Review,* V, 1939-40, pp. 235-241.

Rahv, Philip, "Franz Kafka: The Hero as a Lonely Man", *Kenyon Review,* I, 1939, pp. 60-74.

Warren, Austin, "Kosmos Kafka", *Southern Review,* VII, 1941, pp. 350-365.

Wolff, K., "Franz Kafka", *Southern Review,* VII, 1941-42, pp. 350-365.

Additional Bibliographies

Benson, Ann Thornton, "Franz Kafka: An American Bibliography", *Bulletin of Bibliography,* XXII 1958, pp. 112-114.

Flores, Angel, *Franz Kafka Today,* 1958.

Politzer, Heinz, *Franz Kafka: Parable and Paradox,* 1962.

www.ingramcontent.com/pod-product-compliance
Lightning Source LLC
LaVergne TN
LVHW011720060526
838200LV00051B/2971